Arundhati Roy's
The God of Small Things

CONTINUUM CONTEMPORARIES

Also available in this series

Forthcoming in this series:

· ARUNDHATI ROY'S

The God of Small Things

A READER'S GUIDE

JULIE MULLANEY

CONTINUUM | NEW YORK | LONDON

2002

The Continuum International Publishing Group Inc
370 Lexington Avenue, New York, NY 10017

The Continuum International Publishing Group Ltd
The Tower Building, 11 York Road, London SE1 7NX

www.continuumbooks.com

Printed in the United States of America

Library of Congress Cataloguing-in-Publication Data

Mullaney, Julie.
    Arundhati Roy's The god of small things : a reader's guide / Julie
Mullaney.
        p. cm.
    Includes bibliographical references.
    ISBN 0-8264-5327-9
    1. Roy, Arundhati. God of small things. 2. India—In literature. 3.
Twins in literature. I. Title.
    PR9499.3.R59 G6336 2002
    823'.914—dc21
                                2002000990

ISBN 0-8264-5327-9

Contents

The Novelist

Suzanna Arundhati Roy was born in 1961 and grew up in Ayemenem in the state of Kerala, India. "Home" to what Roy terms "four of the world's great religions: Hinduism, Islam, Christianity and Marxism," Kerala is a historical meeting point between cultures. This is directly reflected in Roy's own inheritance for she is the daughter of a Syrian Christian mother (Mary Roy) and a Bengali Hindu father. Her parents divorced when she and her brother were young. Mary Roy (later and locally a well-known social activist) ran an informal school, Corpus Christi, which Arundhati attended. At sixteen she left home and lived in a squatter's camp in Delhi before taking up an apprenticeship in architecture at the New Delhi School of Architecture. After gaining an honors degree, she worked as a research assistant at the National Institute of Urban Affairs briefly. While there she took a small role in the film *Massey Saab* by director Pradeep Krishen, now her husband. She then took a scholarship to go to Italy to study the restoration of monuments. On returning to India her first professional writing assignment was the commentary for Ashish Chandola's documentary film *How the Rhinoceros Returned*, followed by a 26-part television epic with Krishen called *The Banyan Tree*. She wrote two screenplays: *In Which Annie Gives It Those Ones*, and the Channel Four (UK) feature *Electric Moon* (1992) for which she was also production designer. In an interview Roy argues that these forays into writing were "exercises in limitations" that helped hone her writing before she began *The God of Small Things*, which was she contends "artistically by far the most ambitious thing that I have ever done. When I wrote the book, I was aware that I was trying to do things, to explore ways of thinking that I couldn't as a screenplay writer . . . that brooding, introspective, circular quality of the narrative would have been hard to achieve in cinema."

Prior to *The God of Small Things* she also published a pair of controversial articles, "The Great Indian Rape Trick" (Parts 1 and 11), composed in response to Shekar Kapur's film *Bandit Queen* (1994) and based on the life of the late Phoolan Devi in which Roy charged Kapur with exploiting Devi and misrepresenting both her life and her meaning in wider public discourses. In these articles we can ascertain in the debate about the place and meaning of Phoolan Devi in Indian culture generally, a set of concerns more fully delineated in *The God of Small Things*, primarily focusing on the ways in which Indian women are and have been, historically, situated at the nexus of a variety of intersecting discourses of race, religion, gender, sexuality, caste, and class. Phoolan Devi, born poor and low-caste, was a legendary *dacoit* (bandit) known for raiding villages with her gang and redistributing wealth from upper class, upper-caste landlords to poor villagers. Her notoriety in India grew primarily on the grounds of her alleged murder of a group of upper-caste *thakurs* (landlords) as retaliation for an earlier alleged gang rape by these men. Devi's story came to national attention because of the social, cultural, and political implications of this transgression of caste; a lower-caste *dacoit* woman allegedly attacking upper-caste landed *thakurs*. This earlier confrontation with the intricacies of the caste system has shaped Roy's later discussions of caste in *The God of Small Things*. Caste, and the various histories of complicity and transgression that mark it as a wider system of classification and belonging, are important themes in the novel. The unities and divisions of life in a social system regulated by caste in the face of wider social changes and political movements are explored—specifically in the unravelling tragedy of Ammu, Rahel, Estha, and Velutha—as the "Love Laws," "the laws that lay down who should be loved and how" (p.31).

Roy's writings on Devi can be understood as an act of intervention in a wider debate about the cultural place of Phoolan Devi that surfaced (in India and internationally) centered around the politics of authenticity, agency, authority, and responsibility in the representation of the "real" life experiences and struggles of an individual. Gender and sexuality were at the centre of this controversy since Kapur presents several rape scenes, one of which is a gang rape of Devi, an act Roy suggests aggravated middle-class morality within the Indian public sphere. This controversy was further complicated by Devi's own attempts to stop the film from being distributed and screened in India because although Devi had consented to the making of the film, she had not anticipated the visually graphic representation of rape in the film—a portrayal that as Leela Fernandes suggests "violated her sense of honour in the context of hegemonic social norms in India that depict rape victims as figures of shame and dishonour."

Roy's articles raise crucial questions regarding the political implications of witnessing and representing forms of power and domination that apply to the production, commodification, and distribution of Phoolan Devi's life history on film but also in a wider variety of media including reviews, reportage, (auto)biography, testimonial and legal documents. Drawing attention to the ways in which Devi's access to a viewing of the film had been refused, Roy focuses on the film's location within trans/national material, historical, and political relations of inequality. Roy's own interventions in this debate are part of the wider political economy in which cultural texts are traded and transmitted, and any detailed analysis of her critical writings must subject her narrative of Devi to the same scrutiny. Her championing (after Mala Sen, Devi's biographer) of elements of Devi's life history as examples of subaltern resistance needs careful attention as does her deployment of her access to Devi in her narrative practices, particularly how she narrates the story of her involvement with Devi. Devi's story and Roy's interventions are colored also by the complexities involved in any analysis of the politics of representing the subaltern woman in the global context of multinational cultural production. "Subaltern" is a term derived from the work of Antonio Gramsci and adopted by a well-known group of Indian historians to refer to the suppressed or silenced peasantry. One of the most influential essays in response to the work of the Subaltern Studies group, "Can the Subaltern Speak?" by Gayatri Spivak highlights the positioning of the subaltern woman "even more deeply in shadow" because of the tendency historically to prioritize men in representations of subaltern insurgency. The most potent example of such representations for Spivak is the documentation of *sati* or widow sacrifice in colonial India. While interrogating the archive of Brahmanic codes and texts alongside those on the abolition of sati, Spivak compulsively argues, "between patriarchy and imperialism . . . the figure of the woman disappears . . . into the violent shuttling which is the displaced figuration of the "third world woman" caught between tradition and modernization." In deploying the term 'third world woman' Spivak is referring here to the production in a variety of arenas (latterly first world feminisms) of a specific model of "third world woman," a homogenized and systematized vision of female oppression, which can elide the significant differences between women. Roy in the Devi articles sets out to demonstrate the ways in which the manipulation and narration of Phoolan Devi's story by Kapur is a further example of this production of a homogenous model of "third world woman-hood." In *The God of Small Things*, she takes that critique to another level by offering in a more intricately designed and executed manner the reasons why that narrative of "third world woman" needs to be and is dispelled in her exploration of the separate but overlapping and intricately braided lives of her female protagonists: Mammachi, Baby Kochamma, Ammu, Rahel, and the family cook, Kochu Maria. She carefully delineates not their false homogeneity as representations of oppressed "third world woman" but the range of options and choices, whether complicit, resistant— or both—to the dominant order which structures each of their individual life stories and their relation to the larger tessellations, familial, and cultural histories.

Roy's articles offer important critical readings of some of the ways in which Kapur's film fails to recognize the complexity and variety of Devi's responses and resistances to her life experiences. Roy's main objections to the film are worth elaborating on for the general questions they ask about the relations between truth and fiction, (auto)biography, and the representation of women within the context of national discourses and wider discussions of the subaltern (in postcolonial studies). Roy first tackles what she sees as Kapur's spurious "Truth" claims and his use of those claims to disarm criticism of the film. The problem that arises for Roy is "whether or not it [the film] *is* the Truth is no longer relevant. The point is that it will, (if it hasn't already)—*become* the truth." While she enumerates the various "truth claims" embedded consciously and unconsciously in the film, it is difficult to (now) uphold her statement that Kapur's version of Devi has "*become* the truth" in view of the existence of a number of versions of Devi's story including Mala Sen's biography and Devi's (ghost) "autobiography" *I, Phoolan Devi*.

As Roy herself concedes in a related point the issue is really that "Phoolan Devi the woman has ceased to be important. . . . She's only a version of herself. There are other versions of her that are jostling for attention." That Devi's story exists in multiple forms in sometimes complimentary but often contradictory, contesting, or overlapping versions surely indicates that any *single* claim to Truth is invalidated by the existence of these other versions. It might also suggest that Devi is in more control of the production of her own story than Roy's intervention implies.

One of the questions Roy is really raising in the Devi articles is what responsibility biographers (whether it be Mala Sen or Shekhar Kapur) have to their subjects? The question Roy asks particularly of Kapur's film biography is whether permission given to "cut, alter, and adapt" includes the right to "distort and falsify." This question leads into her second major criticism of Kapur's film, the alleged misuse of Mala Sen's *India's Bandit Queen: The True Story of Phoolan Devi* (1991). For Roy, in Kapur's film "every landmark— every decision, every turning point in Phoolan Devi's life, starting with how she became a dacoit in the first place, has to do with having been raped, or avenging rape." It is then for Roy a film in which "Rape is the main dish. Caste is the sauce that it swims in." By contrast, Sen's book for Roy "tells a different story . . . full of ambiguity, full of concern, full of curiosity about who this woman Phoolan Devi *really* is." Roy's language is interesting here, for it reiterates what is one of the struggles taking place in both articles, the struggle between a concern for justice, that Devi be treated justly, but also more problematically and perhaps revelatory an anxiety about the (desire for the) existence of some *authentic* or essential Devi that can be extricated from the *versions* of Devi's life history or Devi's own *performances* of self already in circulation. For Roy, the usefulness of Sen's biography remains the attention paid to the variety of *reasons* apart from Kapur's alleged singular one as to why Devi acts the way she does toward her life experiences.

The God of Small Things was completed in May 1996, launched in April 1997 in Delhi, and won the *Booker Prize* in London in October 1997. Published in over forty different languages, it has sold over six million copies worldwide and has won Roy global attention and acclaim. After donating the Booker prize money to the Narmada Bachao Andolan, a grassroots activist group opposing further "big dam" development in India, Roy has used the attention brought about by the success of *The God of Small Things* to further awareness of the humanitarian, environmental, and economic fall-out that accompanies development policies from India's entry into the nuclear age to the place of multinationals in the global econ-omy. Eschewing fiction, momentarily at least, Roy has followed *The God of Small Things* with a number of critical essays: "The End of Imagination" (1998) on India's entry into the nuclear age and "The Greater Common Good" (1999), an impassioned indictment of the operations of the World Bank and generations of state and national governments in the continuing development of India's "big dam" projects. Both of these essays have been republished as *The Cost of Living* (1999). The text of Roy's Nehru Lecture given at Cambridge University and her latest essay "The Art of Spinning," also published as "Power Politics" (2000), followed suit. The latter takes on the Texas based multinational company Enron over its alleged activities in the supply of (electric) power to Maharastra. All are representa-tive of Roy's engagement with the local effects of government poli-cies together with the wider issues of international development, globalization, and the mobilization and meaning of local resistances to the capricious operations of the transnational economy. In the central and western states of Mahya Pradesh, Maharasthra, and Gujurat, for example, a series of dams (notably and most publicly in the Narmada Valley) threatens the homes and livelihoods of tens of millions. Roy has joined the Narmada Bachao Andolan and she has protested with, been arrested for, and found herself on court charges over her involvement in political demonstrations against the dams generating much controversy both in India and abroad.

"THE ONLY THING WORTH GLOBALISING IS DISSENT." (ROY)

Globalization can be described as the process whereby individual lives and local communities are affected by economic and cultural forces that operate worldwide. More simply, in effect it is the process of the world becoming a single place. Some attention must be paid to the politics of Roy's engagement with and situation as the public voice of India's anti-globalization movement outside India to the extent that Channel Four News (UK), in a feature entitled "Power Failure," described her as "India's leading globalisation critic" (June 21, 2000). Roy's tackling in her critical work of what she calls the "privatisation and corporatisation (*sic*) of [India's] *essential infrastructure*" is really about what she sees as the ongoing neo-colonizing relationship between the First and Third World. One of the dominant understandings of globalization is that it represents, in the period of rapid decolonization after the World War II, the transmutation of imperialism into the supra-national operation of economics, communications, and culture. Roy sees this as one of the major questions in the current era: "Is globalisation about the eradication of world poverty or is it a mutant variety of colonialism, remote controlled and digitally operated?"

For Roy, India's colonial histories cannot be ignored and the argument that posits globalization as just another permutation of the colonialisms practiced by the Portuguese or the British during their "occupations" of India is the more persuasive. In "The Art of

Spinning," she provides a potent example of how a new generation of Indians are being "groomed" to "man the backroom operations of giant transnational companies" while being effectively "hidden" under the homogenizing and decontextualising influences of the global economy:

They are trained to answer telephone queries from the U.S. and the UK (on subjects ranging from a credit card enquiry to advice about a washing machine). On no account must the caller know that his or her enquiry is being attended to by an Indian, sitting at a desk on the outskirts of Delhi. The Call Centre Colleges train their students in British and American accents. They have to read foreign newspapers so that they can chat about the news or the weather. On duty they have to change their given names. Sushima becomes Susie, Govind becomes Gerry, Advani becomes Andy. They're paid exactly one-tenth of the salaries of their counterparts abroad.

An overt connection can be made here between the operations of the contemporary economy and the recruitment and mobilization of an Indian elite into the Indian Civil Service (ICS), the steel frame of British rule in India in the last century, both groups being essential to the maintenance and administration of empires. However, globalization is not a simple unidirectional movement or flow from the powerful to the weak, from the central to the peripheral, because globalism is transcultural in the same way that imperialism itself has been. More overt recognition has to be given to the variety of ways in which globalization is received and the role of the sending and receiving culture in any transaction. In some contrast to Roy's later critical articles which tend to oscillate between focusing on globalization as a result of top-down dominance to recognizing it more broadly as a transcultural process in which both individuals and local communities actively appropriate and transform for their own uses and contexts inherited models, *The God of Small Things* itself contains a more alert and detailed, if indirect, exploration of the *variety* of strategies deployed by the receiving as of the sending culture in its transactions with a global culture. In this, *The God of Small Things* is concerned with the resemblances *between* how individuals, groups, or local communities engage with the forces of globalization and how they might have engaged and appropriated the forces of imperial dominance historically. More generally, Roy's engagement with the politics of globalization offers us an interesting overview or case study of the ways in which certain national governments along with international organizations like the World Bank and the IMF (International Monetary Fund) are complicit in the organization, execution, and maintenance of new imperialisms.

Like the Caribbean writer Jamaica Kincaid before her who successfully capitalized on the attention garnered by her prose fictions to publish *A Small Place* (1997), a devastating critique of the prostitution of another former colony, Antigua, Roy has used both the success of *The God of Small Things* and the critical work which has followed it to capture wider media attention for the political issues that interest her. There are shared ecocritical threads in both the fiction and the criticism. In *The God of Small Things* the once powerful river, the Meenachal, lifeblood and livelihood of all the people, previously imbued with the "power to evoke fear" and to "change lives" has had its "teeth drawn." Ongoing unsustainable and damaging man-made environmental changes ensure the river now bears the character of a death mask reduced to "a slow sludging green ribbon lawn that ferried fetid garbage to the sea." "Upstream," Roy continues, "clean mothers washed clothes and pots in unadulterated factory effluents. . . . Further inland . . . a five-star hotel chain had bought the Heart of Darkness" (p. 125). The subjugation of a great river and the transformation of "History" into the more aesthetically pleasing and marketable "Heritage" detailed in Roy's narration of the afterlives or "Toy Histories" of "The History House" is also relentlessly documented in *The Cost of Living* and *Power Politics* as the fallout from India's continued subjugation to the demands of transnational capital and the global tourism industry, and its wayward commitment to the execution of Nehru's vision of "big dams" as the saving graces, the "new temples of modern India."

While her critical work has usefully drawn attention to a variety of local and often more specifically feminist interventions in glob-alization and eco-critical debates, she has faced much criticism within India from both sides of the political divide, notably from the historian Ramachandra Guha for her writing as well as her personal support of these issues. It is important to be alert to the variety of ways in which Roy's situation abroad as *the* public voice of a movement that is, perhaps, more fractured and diverse in its aims and objectives than at first appears, can unwittingly and indi-rectly elide the voices, activities, contributions, and diverse opinions of others, but it is equally crucial to recognize the way in which this work (in fiction as in critical essay) speaks for and to those who dissent while facilitating or furthering the challenges or awareness of, for example, local resistances. Roy herself characterizes her in-terventions in the current debates about globalization and India as the mobilization of a "politics of opposition": "The only way to keep power on a tight leash is to oppose it, never to seek to own it or have it. Opposition is permanent." She is, however, aware of the ways in which fate has conspired to make her voice heard and the concomitant dangers of living under the illusion that this automati-cally translates as the ability to orchestrate and deliver great changes.

ROY AND INDO-ANGLIAN WRITING

The God of Small Things can be set in the wider tradition of what is often called Indo-Anglian writing, one of several terms for Indian writing written in English. The tradition of Indian writing in English stems from the late eighteenth century, but spread first after its establishment as *the* language of the Indian Civil Service and thus of the administration and maintenance of Empire. However, the rise of the Indian novel in English is linked particularly to the generation of authors writing in the 1930s which included Raja Rao, Mulk Raj Anand, G.V Desani, and later perhaps the most well known, R.K Narayan, for his chronicles of Malgudi (an imaginary town in Mysore at the center of his portraits of an India caught between tradition and modernity). Followed by writers as various as V.S Naipaul, Nayantara Sahgal, A.K. Ramunujan, Kamala Das, Anita Desai, Amitav Ghosh, Salman Rushdie, Vikram Chandra, Upamanyu Chatterjee, Rohinton Mistry, Amit Chaudhuri, and Gita Mehta, the boundaries of the term Indo-Anglian are somewhat porous applying to those writers permanently resident in India and Pakistan but also including writers of the Indian diaspora in, for example, Britain, America, Canada, and the Caribbean. Indo-Anglian fiction is largely a transnational, diasporic phenomenon, the product of complex collisions and/or as some critics like Harish Trivedi or Graham Huggan would have it, "collusions" between East and West.

From its beginnings Indian writing in English has been placed in a complex and often conflicted relation with the other languages and literatures of the subcontinent such as Hindi, Tamil, Marathi, Malayalam, Kannada, or Urdu. Thomas Macaulay's famous "Minute on Indian Education" of 1835, the template for the cultural project of the British in India, proclaimed with little justification or knowledge of either "Sanskrit or Arabic" that a "single shelf of a good European library was worth the whole native literature of India and Arabia." More recently, pronouncing about Indo-Anglian rather than "European" literature particularly, Salman Rushdie stoked the fires when he suggested, in his "Introduction" to *The Vintage Book of Indian Writing 1947–1997* that the body of writing produced in the fifty and more years since Independence by "those Indian writers *working in English* is proving to be a stronger and more important body of work than most of what has been produced in the 16 official languages of India." He continues to argue that this "new, and still burgeoning, Indo-Anglian literature represents perhaps the most valuable contribution India has yet made to the world of books." It must be noted that this is Rushdie throwing down the gauntlet as a response to several charges laid at the feet of Indian writers in English, particularly, but not always, from critics of Indo-Anglian writing inside India.

Most ignominious of these charges for Rushdie is the often reiterated belief "for some" that "English-language Indian writing will never be more than a post-colonial anomaly, the bastard child of Empire, sired on India by the departing British; its continuing use of the old colonial tongue [is] seen as a fatal flaw that renders it forever inauthentic." Rushdie is overstating the case somewhat in the name of rhetoric. The reasons for the contested place of English in India are more various than he allows and have as much to do with the class privilege historically of its users as the fact of its use. While as Rushdie acknowledges English is the legacy of the British in India, India itself has undergone waves of colonization after the accession of Babur and the Mughal Empire through Portuguese and latterly British occupation. Each of these invasions shaped the development of and relations between India's many languages, although the ramifications proceeding from the introduction of English have received greater attention. In post Independence India, English was designated an associate official language but it has expanded on its earlier (class) base as *the* language of government and is now one of *many* Indian languages. This is not to say there is equability between the languages, hierarchies continue to exist that structure the relationships between India's languages but it is crucial to remain alert to the fact that Indians have lived in many languages simultaneously for thousands of years. As Roy's fellow Indo-Anglian writer, Vikram Chandra, proclaims:

English was everywhere in the world I grew up in and continues to be an inextricable thread in the texture of every day [life]. Along with many other languages, it is spoken in the slums, on the buses and in the post offices and the police stations and courtrooms. English has been spoken and written in on the Indian subcontinent for a few hundred years now, certainly longer than the official and literary Hindu that is our incompletely national language.(p.8)

Chandra and Rushdie also tackle a second common accusation leveled at Indian writers who choose to write in English by their critics; that English in India is inadequate to express "Indianness," that it is "inauthentic." This is a maneuvre often rhetorically tied to the setting of Indo-Anglian writing in opposition to "Regional Writing" which then allows its critics, like Harish Trivedi, to argue that as a literature Indian writing in English is predominantly characterised by a metropolitan or cosmopolitan elitism which produces a literature increasingly written by and for the English-knowing alone. Chandra explains the psychology of this manoeuver in the following way:

The attempt to locate 'Indianness' in 'regional writing' is inevitably problematic, since — in a nation battling numerous secessionist movements — regional specificity is inevitably in conflict with generalized national traits. But 'regional writing' is always connected to the soil, to 'Real India'. And when it's opposed to 'Indo-Anglian writing', the term 'regional writing' implies that writing in English is not regional, that it's pan-Indian, or, worse, cosmopolitan, belonging to nowhere and everywhere.(p.7)

The charges of deracination outlined by Chandra have been contested by writers as early as Raja Rao and as recently as Rushdie, who together reassert the hybrid and pliable nature of Indian English as a tool for the communication of what it might mean to be Indian. For Rao in his foreword to *Kanthapura* (1938) the challenge for the fledgling Indian writer in English is to "convey in a language that is not one's own the spirit that is one's own." "We cannot," Rao continues, "write like the English. We should not. We cannot write only as Indians. We have grown to look at the large world as part of us." For Rao, Indian English will be both local and global, it will recognize in the colors, salts, and tones of its existences that India itself is a hybrid creation, part of the larger world, a conglomeration of what was brought in from outside, absorbed and reworked, and what was there. In turn, whatever Rushdie's controversial claims for the canon of Indo-Anglian writing, he has never been shy in acknowledging the debt his writing owes to the rhythms, patterns, habits of thought, and metaphor of his Indian tongues and how they shape his use of English. "There is not, need not be, should not be" he contends "an adversarial relationship between English-language literature and the other literatures of India. We drink from the same well, India, that inexhaustible horn of plenty, nourishes us all." Chandra in turn rejects the purism that argues that to be an Indian writer means effectively choosing the one over the many. He confirms not just the validity of Indian English as a means of personal and cultural expression but also as a form of memorializing when he argues:

A language is a living thing. A patois born in soldiers' camps not so long ago became Urdu, whose beauty ravishes our hearts. To love Urdu for her low origins and her high refinements, for her generous heart and her reckless love, is not to give up Punjabi. What a mean economy of love and belonging it must be, in which one love is always traded in for another, in which a heart is so small that it can only contain one *jannat*, one heaven. [...] I write in English, and I have forgotten nothing, and I have given up nothing. And I know the tastes and quirks and nuances of my regional audience ... as well or better than any Bengali poet knows her regional audience.(pp.8-9)

The arguments about the politics of language use articulated and delineated by Rushdie and Chandra are crucial for an understanding of Roy's language(s) and their political contexts in *The God of Small Things*. While Roy speaks Malayalam and Hindi, English is, in spite of its contentiousness, her primary language. As she has noted in interviews, she may dip into her other languages, but she couldn't write a story in them. In *The God of Small Things*, her "wrenching" of the English language from its colonial roots through a series of "collaged words, regional aphorisms and culturally eclipsed meanings" creating in the process what Taisha Abraham calls "her own 'Locusts Stand I' " has led Aijaz Ahmad to conclude that "Roy is the first Indian writer in English where a marvellous stylistic resource becomes available for provincial, vernacular culture without any effect of exoticism or estrangement, and without the book reading as translation."

The tradition of Indo-Anglian writing to which Roy belongs is a many-headed creature and has evolved several different, and by no means immediately identifiable, literary styles across the spectrum from realism to fabulism. Jon Mee's important essay "After Midnight: The Indian novel in English of the 80s and 90s" (*Postcolonial Studies*, 1998) takes as its starting point the publication of Rushdie's *Midnight's Children* (1981) and how it has been seen in a somewhat exaggerated manner as a turning point which single-handedly brought about a renaissance in contemporary Indian writing in English. Like *The God of Small Things*, Rushdie's novel won the Booker prize in 1981 but it was also awarded the commemorative Booker of Bookers in 1993 and has been widely acclaimed as one of the foremost English language novels of its generation. Its impact generally has been in no small part due to its engagement with what are often considered wider postmodern and postcolonial concerns. It is postmodern in the sense that *Midnight's Children* actively encourages us to reconsider our understanding of what "History" is and where it may be found while more generally questioning the form of the historical novel itself by noting the impossibility of, for example, categorizing our experience of the world without generalization or omission. In the process, Rushdie is drawing our attention to the necessity of embracing the stories embedded or elided within that singular factual linear narrative we conventionally call "History." As Rushdie's narrator, Saleem, pronounces: "[T]here are so many stories to tell, too many, such an excess of intertwined lives events miracles places rumours, so dense a commingling of the improbable and the mundane! I have been a swallower of lives and to know me, just the one of me, you'll have to swallow the lot as well." Rushdie's project in *Midnight's Children* can be understood as postcolonial because it actively revisits and interrogates India's colonial histories and its postcolonial imaginings through a critical examination of the promises and failures of the post-colonial state. Epic in its ambition and form and part historical metafiction, part magical realism, *Midnight's Children* charts the divergent fates of the children of Independence while uncovering the intertwining social, historical, and religious roots of the nation, roots which always threaten to fissure rather than anchor the post-Independence state.

Its author has also been placed alongside a new generation of writers (many British based) like Timothy Mo, Ian McEwan, Kazuo Ishiguro, Angela Carter, Martin Amis, and J.G. Ballard who together have redefined the boundaries and concerns of the post-war

"British" novel in light of the decline of Britain as a world power in the aftermath of Empire. The influence of *Midnight's Children* on the work of a new generation of Indo-Anglian writers including Roy is apparent in numerous ways and has been summarized by Mee: "[T]he appearance of a certain postmodern playfulness, the turn to history, a new exuberance of language, the reinvention of allegory, the sexual frankness, even the prominent references to Bollywood [in the work of contemporary Indo-Anglian writers] all seem to owe something to Rushdie's novel." As Mee acknowledges, to attribute the regeneration of a tradition to a single novel without looking at the internal social and cultural changes in post-Independence India that have facilitated the wider regeneration of Indo-Anglian writing is short sighted. Among these, we must include the deterioration in the post-Independence state of adherence to consensus politics and the idea of "unity *within*" central to both the nationalist struggle and the post-Independence state under and after Jawaharlal Nehru, the rise and fall and rise again of Indira Gandhi (Prime Minister 1966–77, 1980–84), and the influence on the public and private imagination of the state of Emergency (1975–1977). Each of these events initiated a questioning of the politics and values of the new state, a wider subject of debate in India's many languages and literatures, and in Indo-Anglian writing *prior* to *Midnight's Children* generally and *not just* in Rushdie's vivid dissection of the various fates of the children of Midnight.

While it is on one level easy to see why Rushdie's multifaceted national allegory (what Frederic Jameson terms the most character-istic form of the postcolonial novel) detailing the fragmented and hybrid histories of the nation has been situated as *the* Indo-Anglian novel to regenerate a tradition, to situate *Midnight's Children* in this way is also to do some injustice to those extant chroniclers of Independent India like Nayantara Sahgal or Anita Desai with whom Roy's work shares much. If Rushdie is the most routinely identified influence (in terms of form, structure, language, and the desire to hold up to wider public scrutiny the perforated sheet of the nation), the work of Nayantara Sahgal and Anita Desai indicates that Roy shares with them a familiar set of concerns. These are notably a focus on the intermingling of public and private histories and the situation of women at the nexus of a variety of overlapping and sometimes contesting discourses of gender, sexuality, religion, caste, and citizenship. Like Sahgal's *A Situation in New Delhi* (1977), which narrates the tragic fallout from a relationship between an Indian minister and an English journalist against the background of the Naxalite uprising in India in the late 1960s and the early 1970s, or her *Rich Like Us* (1983), which details the relationship between a working-class Englishwoman Rose and her Indian "husband," Roy's novel is studded with relationships across the divides of race, class, caste, and nationality like that between Chacko and Margaret or Ammu and Velutha. The events of *The God of Small Things*, like Sahgal's *A Situation in New Delhi*, are also partially narrated against the background of the Naxalite uprisings which started in West Bengal but the tremors of which are felt in Roy's Kerala at an important point in its flirtation with Marxism.

Equally, the portraits of Roy's women in *The God of Small Things* recall both Sahgal's and Desai's work including the latter's quietly ominous *Fire on the Mountain* (1977) and *Clear Light of Day* (1980) through to the most recent *Fasting, Feasting* (1999), which together paint a devastating critique of the interwoven choices and fates facing generations of Indian women in light of the inherited dominant mythic archetypes of Indian womanhood (like Sita, Draupadi, Durga, Parvati, and Lakshmi) the cornerstones on which, as Desai indicates, the Indian family and therefore Indian society is built. In tandem with Rushdie in parts of *Shame* (1983) and *Midnight's Children* and Anita Desai and Githa Hariharan in *Fire on the Mountain* and *The Thousand Faces of Night* (1992) respectively, Roy chooses to narrate her tale partially through the child's eye point of view, which allows her to tell her story from both sides of the divide — from inside and outside the dominant matrix, through an examination of the ways in which the child receives, molds and is molded by the values, beliefs, ways of doing and being handed down by the adults in their world. It also allows Roy to chart the ways in which the children imbibe and/or contest these narratives as they move through life. Given that the novel is really an exploration of the historical tensions and conflicts associated with the particularities of the children's caste, class, religious, and gender inheritances, the child's eye view and the focus on the child's sense of fear, enchantment, innocence, exaggeration, fascination, and disappointment allows Roy to look again at the world *as if* it were "new minted."

Like Rushdie, Sahgal, and Desai, Roy is interested in excavating and reclaiming the hidden histories buried under the homogenizing myth of the nation in the post-Independence years. Like Desai's portrait of devastation and its disquieting survivals in the Old Delhi of *Clear Light of Day* (1980), Roy adumbrates not just the moment of tragedy but the responses to it in the afterlives of her protagonists. More specifically, her chosen era is the late 1960s between perhaps the two most traumatic events of India's twentieth century history; Independence/Partition and the state of Emergency inaugurated by Indira Gandhi. Roy's focus is trained then on the more obviously *inbetween* moments in the nation's public history: when the world's attention is elsewhere, and when a variety of internal social, cultural, and political forces are in foment. It is noteworthy given the novel's obsession with the small in relation to the large that Roy chooses to more obviously excavate the personal and the local rather than the wider public and national canvas directly. Notwithstanding the attention to the *small*, the *personal*, and the *local specificities* of *place*, Roy's novel can be read also as *national allegory*, because of its wider exploration of the hybrid nature of India and its cultural origins. If Mumbai stands in Rushdie's *Midnight's Children* as the supreme signifier of the inherent hybridity and multiplicity of the nation, Kerala functions in a similar way in Roy's text. While the novel travels back and forth between past and present, the prime focus is on the dislocations effected in those quieter moments by the calamitous friction created when "four of the world's greatest religions: Christianity, Hinduism, Marxism and Islam" meet under Kerala's intemperate skies.

Outside of the inferred influence of the tradition of Indo-Anglian writing as exemplified by Rushdie, Sahgal, Desai, and Narayan, the influence of James Joyce, Rudyard Kipling, D.H. Lawrence, William Faulkner, F. Scott Fitzgerald, and Vladimir Nabokov have all been variously attributed and acknowledged by critics and by Roy herself. For Michael Gorra, writing in *The London Review of Books* (1997), there are obvious connections between Roy and Faulkner. First, both Faulkner and Roy are keen to focus on the specificities of the local place. Because of "its story of sex and sudden death, transgression and familial decay *The God of Small Things* could be seen as the first Indian attempt at Southern Gothic." For Gorra, that surface similarity is furthered in Roy's "concentration on a past that can't be smoothed over, a history with which one has to go on living" and in the structural complexity of Roy's novel: "Its third-person narration doesn't present the same sentence-by-sentence difficulties as Faulkner's interior monologues, but . . . nevertheless displays . . . the same split between the order of the narrative and the order of the events it describes."

While Roy is somewhat impatient, and understandably so, with the comparisons with Faulkner, admitting she has never read his work, she does allow that having read other writers from the American South like Mark Twain and Harper S. Lee "there's an infusion or intrusion of landscape in their literature that might be similar to mine." Her attention to the specificities of space and place and her determination to carve a space on the literary map for Kerala and its cultural histories is most often the basis for the ongoing comparison with Joyce and Faulkner. "I wanted," argues Roy "to drive my stake in here [in Kerala]. I wanted to say that this is my place, that it deserves literature. It was very important to me that it be real, these stars, these leaves." Roy's regional specificity has been a focus of much comment. For Gorra, "what's immediately refreshing" about Roy's Kerala is its "difference" from what he suggests are the "familiar settings of most Indian novels, from the baked and friable land of the North or the crackle and pop of Bombay." Rosemary Dinnant reiterates the allure of Roy's "exotic setting" in "tropical Marxist Kerala" yet it must be acknowledged that Roy's portrait of the region offers a rather different lens from which to view Kerala, one some distance from the pastoral fables of that other great chronicler of the Indian South, R.K. Narayan.

2

The Novel

RETURNS

The *God of Small Things* opens with a return journey by one of its central protagonists, Rahel, from America to Ayemenem, in the southern state of Kerala, India. Return journeys are an organizing theme of the novel through which Roy explores a matrix of social and cultural anxieties. This physical act of return facilitates other returns. Emotionally and psychologically, Rahel revisits the tessellations of family and family history and in doing so reopens India's colonial and post-colonial histories to new scrutiny. Weaving between past and present, most obviously the 1960s and the early 1990s but with some casting glances across centuries of Indian history, the novel traces in an episodic manner tragic events in the childhood of Rahel and her twin Estha; namely the accidental drowning of their English cousin Sophie Mol and the less than accidental death of their mother's lower-caste lover, Velutha. Although the death of Sophie Mol and Velutha takes place on the same day, the novel traces the series of events in the fortnight previous and relates their repercussions into the 1990s, the point of Rahel's return. In the process it explores the topography of the Ipe family and the subterranean connections between individual family history and local, national, and world histories. The tragic events in Ayemenem are, for example, narrated against the background of the brief return to power of Kerala's second state Communist government in the 1960s under the flamboyant E.M.S. Namboodiripad which itself operates under the shadows thrown by wider events and conflicts of the period like the Vietnam War and the moon landing. The elements of the story set in 1969 are primarily narrated through the eyes of seven-year-old twins, Rahel and Estha, while the tragic repercussions in the present are narrated through the adult Rahel.

Rahel returns to Ayemenem, ostensibly to visit Estha who for the first time in twenty three years has himself returned to the family home. Estha had been banished to live with their father in Calcutta in the aftermath of the deaths of Sophie Mol and Velutha, after being forced to falsely indict their mother's lover for the manufactured crime of kidnapping the children and what is seen by the family and community as the real social crime of an affair with their mother, Ammu. An impassioned exploration of blood and belonging unfolds as the novel retraces the tangled web of desires, conflicts, alliances, frustrations, and betrayals that characterizes the build up to those early tragic events that lead to the break up of the family.

Estha and Rahel's family are from the beginning characterized as on the edge of the dominant order of society in Kerala in the 1960s. This vulnerable situation on the margins is signaled to the reader in two significant ways. First of all, the twins are brought up in a family that is of Syrian Christian ancestry, although they have a Bengali Hindu father, which means as their astringent Grand Aunt Baby Kochamma points out, that they are "Half-Hindu hybrids whom no self-respecting Syrian Christian would ever marry" (p. 45).

Syrian-Christians are a sizeable minority with a long history in Kerala but less so with regards to the predominantly Hindu status quo installed in the post-Independence India painted by Roy. As children of mixed ancestry and divorced parents Rahel and Estha fall between traditions (Hindu and Syrian Christian) and are afforded no real recognition or what the novel calls "Locusts Stand I" (legal standing). This point is signaled by their mother's ongoing refusal to confer on the twins a surname. Estha notes how it is "postponed for the Time Being, while Ammu chose between her husband's name and her father's" (p. 156). This means that the twins are in effect unclaimed (except by their mother) and nameless. One's name is an index of one's identity and the instability of naming, what Rahel identifies as a "more general difficulty" that the family has with "classification" (p. 31) as such indicates that there are certain fissures or gaps in the twins' identity.

The children's "confusion" about their own identity is marked out early in the novel by the very fact of their compound entity: "Esthappen and Rahel thought of themselves together as Me, and separately, individually, as We or Us. As though they were a rare breed of Siamese twins, physically separate, but with joint identities" (p. 2). This general confusion is further compounded in a family situation replete with exuberant play on names and identities. The "Baby" in *Baby* Kochamma, for example, ostensibly relating to her diminutive stature, comes to describe her general stagnation and failure to go forward in life, marked by her inordinate and lifelong attachment to the impossibly attainable Father Mulligan. At the same time, the pet name masks her real name, Navomi Ipe, and thus part of her independent identity. The twins themselves are conferred with or take on a whole host of names, each of which accretes heightened significance as the story unfolds, names that simultaneously reveal and mask elements of their real or assumed identities. The damaging nature of this fissure in the twins' identity is poignantly reiterated in their desire to claim as surrogate father figures both their Uncle Chacko and Velutha, their mother's lover. Interestingly, the twins' (failed) attempt to claim Chacko is played out in a battle over names; what he will and will not allow them to call him. If naming is a site of anxiety for the children, the protean quality of the children's many names offers a space for the subversion of inherited models of identity and kinship. When Velutha reaches out across the boundaries of caste to the children he does so by openly "conspiring" with and extending the exuberant play on names and the mobility of identities in his renaming of Estha, "Esthappappychachen Kuttappen Peter Mon . . . [a name that] became a delighted, breathless, Rumplestilskin-like dance among the rubber trees"(p. 191).

At this stage also, the twins general confusion and emotional vulnerability is underwritten in their absorption in the stories read to them by the twin architects of their fates — their mother Ammu and their Grand Aunt Baby Kochamma. They are fascinated with Rudyard Kipling's *The Jungle Book* (1894–5) and the story of the man-cub Mowgli, caught between the competing claims of the tiger Shere Khan and the other Jungle creatures, but *also* between those of the animal world and Man. Indeed, the code words — "We be of one blood, ye and I" — which ensures Mowgli's safe passage *between* the Jungle worlds of bird, beast, and snake — becomes one of the twins' signature phrases in the novel, replete with their own anxieties, desires, and claims about their own place *in* and *between* worlds (India, England and America, Christianity and Hinduism). Equally, the inherited attachment via Baby Kochamma to the figure of Ariel from *The Tempest* in *Lamb's Tales from Shakespeare* (1807) offers the twins another model of fraught allegiances. Ariel is passed like the twins between parent figures, from mistress to master, from Sycorax to Prospero, and the line from Ariel's song — "Where the bee sucks, there suck I" — is another of the twins often repeated phrases reiterating in the process the novel's focus on intertwining fates where Ammu's sipping of the forbidden flower, in her cross-caste relationship with Velutha effectively shapes not just her own but the collective future.

Second, the family are on the edge because in post-Independence India generally and communist Kerala specifically, the Ipes are remnants of the old colonial elite. They are descendants of that class of persons whom Macaulay predicted in his "Minute on Indian Education" (1857) would be the backbone of the project of administering and maintaining Britain's Indian Empire. This class would be, for Macaulay, "Indian in blood and colour, but English in opinions, in morals and in intellect [and would act as] interpreters between [the British] and the millions whom [they] govern." The Ipe family are the descendents then of those Indians who were part of the steel frame of British rule in India, the Indian Civil Service, most potently represented in the text by Estha and Rahel's grandfather, Benann John Ipe, familiarly known as Pappa-chi, who once claimed, we learn, the grand title of Imperial Ento-mologist. His job of collecting, preserving, and indexing India's fauna for the colonial archive, puts him at the heart of the colonial enterprise. On the one hand, Pappachi fulfills this role as inter-preter; as entomologist he *translates* India *for* the world. On the other hand, his role in translating India represented by his discovery of a new species of moth is like the Indian Civil Service after the departure of the British, *translated* or transformed over time. In the same way that the whirlwind of post-Independence creates a space for the evolution of new and alternate social orders and dynamics of power (Communism, Marxism) that threaten to transform the role of his class generally, the specific rearrangement of the classi-fying systems in Pappachi's chosen profession, entomology, trans-forms and eclipses his role in the discovery of a new species of moth. In line with the novel's engagement with the politics of

naming and identity, Pappachi too is *translated* with the departure
of the British, from "Imperial Entomologist" to *"Joint* Director,
Entomology"(p. 48, my italics), a title in itself revelatory of the new
orders installed after India's Independence and Partition into the
independent states of India and Pakistan from which, in turn, East
Pakistan secedes to form yet another new state, Bangladesh, in 1971.

In Roy's Kerala in 1969, amid the general flourishing of Communist sentiment, the tremors from the Naxalite revolt of peasant
against the old *zamindar* (landlord) class begun in the Northern
state of West Bengal in 1967 are felt further south. Amidst this new
social ferment, the Ipe family still sporting the outmoded and ill-
fitting armor of their imperial connections like Uncle Chacko (with
his Oxford education, his "Balliol oar" and his "Reading Aloud
voice") or Baby Kochamma (with her attachment to Shakespeare
over Mao) are socially and financially vulnerable, threatened with
still further eclipse. Chacko, like Pappachi before him, finds himself
caught between masters, between the newly independent India represented by Mammachi's "Paradise Pickles & Preserves" and the
model of England and Englishness inherited via Pappachi and his
own Oxford education. He is caught between an India seemingly
in revolt *against* tradition as represented also by the popularity of
new ideologies (Communism, Marxism) and a now imagined England, first imbibed through and represented *by* tradition, by his
elite education. Chacko's habitation of or movement between what
are opposing visions and identities is both troubled and insecure.
Like Pappachi, his attempts to take up and maintain a position in
either camp, tradition (England), or modernity (India), resituates
him on the margins of both.

This insecurity is heightened in his acts of impersonation, in his
melodramatic donning of what the children call his "Reading Aloud
Voice." It is instantly comparable with the kinds of impersonation
suggested by the photograph of Pappachi in pride of place in the

Ayemenem house during the twins' childhood. In this, Pappachi's role in the colonial project as Macaulay's Minuteman is always and already rendered problematic:

In the photograph [Pappachi] had taken care to hold his head high enough to hide his double chin, yet not so high as to appear haughty. His light brown eyes were polite, yet maleficent as though he was making an effort to be civil to the photographer while plotting to murder his wife. He had a little fleshy knob on the centre of his upper lip that dropped down over his lower lip in a sort of effeminate pout—the kind that children who suck their thumbs develop. [. . .] He wore khaki jodhpurs though he had never ridden a horse in his life . . . An ivory handled crop lay neatly across his lap. (p. 51)

First of all, the photograph is a way of looking, a generalized representation of Pappachi as colonial subject. As such it suggests how in the discourse of colonialism, colonized subjects are split between contrary positions. Discourse here refers to the structures of thinking that dominate how the colonizers imagine colonial subjects and their relations with them. One such structure of thinking is the stereotype. The colonial stereotype works to establish and maintain the authority of the colonizers while fixing the colonial subject in a particular set of relations with the colonizer. As Homi Bhabha reiterates in *The Location of Culture* (1994):

The objective of colonial discourse is to construe the colonised as a population of degenerate types on the basis of racial origin, in order to justify conquest and to establish systems of administration and instruction . . . colonial discourse produces the colonised as a social reality which is at once an "other" yet entirely knowable and visible. (p. 70)

On the one hand, Pappachi outwardly embodies the "entirely knowable and visible" colonial subject Macaulay proposes, in his khaki jodhpurs and his ivory handled crop. On the other hand, the evidently strained nature of Pappachi's performance reveals that his mimicry is an anxious and ambivalent one because the colonial stereotype *also* stages him as always and already antithetical to the colonizer; childlike, immature, weak, lacking in authority; all of which variously situate him as "Other."

Not withstanding the omnipresent shadow cast by Pappachi across family history as represented by Rahel's fear of "Pappachi's moth," it is Chacko who brings home to both children the real impact of the epistemic violence associated with India's colonization. Epistemic violence refers to the way in which colonialism attacks and shapes the colonized culture's ways of knowing itself, its value systems, ideas, and its relations with the world. Chacko, in his dissection of Pappachi's particular brand of "Anglophilia," offers a lens through which we can see how this epistemic violence operates:

Chacko said that the correct word for people like Pappachi was *Anglophile*. He made Rahel and Estha look up *Anglophile* in the *Reader's Digest Great Encyclopaedic Dictionary*. It said *Person well disposed to the English*. Then Estha and Rahel had to look up *disposed* . . . Chacko said that in Pappachi's case it meant (2) *Bring mind into certain state*. Which, Chacko said, meant that Pappachi's mind had been *brought into a state* which made him like the English (p. 52)

What Chacko and Roy are at pains to illustrate is the way in which colonialism enabled a forced restructuring of relationships and knowledges that worked to split the colonized subject from his/her culture, leaving his/her relationship with the colonizing culture anxious and insecure. The anxieties displayed in the description of Pappachi's photograph and particularly the effort required for him to inhabit, however insecurely, the identity of Macaulayan Minuteman, further underlines the violence integral to the process. This violence is then relayed in the beatings taken by Mammachi and Ammu at the hands of Pappachi, summed up in Ammu's remembrance of her own flogging with the same whip Pappachi flourishes in his photograph (p. 181). What this illustrates is that what happens to the individual has, in Roy's text, distinct and indeed often catastrophic ramifications for the family and wider community. Eclipsed and embittered, Pappachi remains to the end, as Ammu notes, "an incurable CCP, which was short for *chhi-chhi poach* and in Hindi meant shit-wiper." When Ammu leaves her husband because he wishes her to license the plantation manager's sexual requests, Pappachi refuses to believe her story: "[H]e didn't believe that an Englishman, *any* Englishman, would covet another man's wife." (p. 42). Pappachi has so internalized the values, beliefs, and ideologies of the colonizer that he cannot countenance criticism or question of anyone he sees as representative of that system.

Chacko, who on the one hand, cannily dissects the roots of his father's Anglophilia, is on the other hand unable to exorcise himself of his own dream England and his life as a Rhodes scholar where he revels in the freedoms and the enthusiasms afforded by an elite education. Once out of Oxford, Chacko cannot *translate* or accommodate himself to the changing worlds around him, whether it is the responsibilities that come with his marriage to Margaret or his return to an India in flux. He remains stuck in an Oxford that Roy, like Amit Chaudhuri in *Afternoon Raag* (1993), constructs as dream-like; endlessly rehearsing in his reading aloud voice that enchanted period of "Love. Madness. Hope. Infinite Joy"(p. 118). Like Pappachi he is a man out of time. Once Mammachi's liberator, on his return to Ayemenem via Madras, he becomes her tormentor. Chacko removes from Mammachi what was hers alone; the "factory" that is at this stage no more than a large kitchen and nameless. He promptly takes over and in Adamic fashion, names it

"Paradise Pickles & Preserves." Once installed in the factory, he sees no conflict between his ostensible championing of rights for the workers with his sexual exploitation of the factory secretaries. As Ammu is quick to point out, Chacko's self-proclaimed Marxism also fails to *translate*. "Just a case of a spoiled princeling playing *Comrade! Comrade!* An Oxford avatar of the old zamindar mentality—a landlord forcing his attentions on women who depended on him for their livelihood" (p. 65). Chacko, in his grief, and rather like his father before him, abuses his position in the family. He refuses to recognize that as in his love affair with Oxford and Margaret, Ammu too is caught in an enchanted moment with Velutha. On the death of Sophie Mol, he assumes the role of vengeful brother and while not exactly orchestrating the banishment of Ammu and Estha, he does little to stop it before fleeing the family and India altogether in his move to Canada. There he reinvents himself somewhat as an antiques dealer, the irony of which is not lost on the reader. His new occupation reiterates the extent to which he continues to trade in the past and its relics.

This precarious edge of the dominant order on which the family rest, can, as Ammu and her children find out, be a place of liberation; it can offer a space for experiment, to explore alternate options and try out new identities. However, this experimentation and the pushing of inherited boundaries and categorizations can equally be a catastrophic experience as both the Ipe and Paapen family discover in that fateful fortnight in 1969; the moment when as Roy suggests "Edges, Borders, Boundaries, Brinks and Limits" begin to appear on the "horizon" and make their "size and shape" known (p. 3). This is the crux of the novel as indicated by its title—*The God of Small Things*—which sets out to retrace how the size and shape of the known world can change in a day. The novel asks how the small events, the accidents, omissions, calculations, and betrayals of everyday individual histories—the small things—relate to the larger God, the wider order and pattern of life? What happens when "personal turmoil" drops by "at the wayside shrine of the vast, violent, circling, driving, ridiculous, insane, unfeasible, public turmoil of a nation" (p. 19)?

POSTCOLONIAL ARCHAEOLOGIES

The excavation of these relations between the small and the large, the private and the public, governs the ostensible plot of *The God of Small Things*, focused as it is on a teasing out of the fragile threads which link family, community, and nation. It is also what governs its approach to what Roy describes as India's more "public turmoil," its fractured and fractious history across several centuries. In her approach to public as to private history, Roy's approach can best be described as archaeological:

Perhaps it's true that things can change in a day. A few dozen hours can affect the outcome of whole lifetimes . . . when they do, those few dozen hours, like the salvaged remains of a burned house — the charred clock, the singed photograph, the scorched furniture — must be *resurrected from the ruins and examined. Preserved. Accounted for.* Little events, ordinary things, smashed and *reconstituted. Imbued with new meaning. Suddenly they become the bleached bones of a story.* [My italics] (pp. 32/3)

Just as the archaeologist must resurrect and sift through the buried remains to put together a narrative of the past, so Roy excavates and rearranges the scattered shards of family history in order to unlock the wider pattern or order they suggest. For in the moment of crisis or catastrophe itself, there is only "incoherence. As though meaning had slunk out of things and left them fragmented. Disconnected" (p. 225). What I am calling Roy's archaeological approach to "History" itself attempts to bring together contrasting ways of looking at how we attempt to know and understand the past, represented on the one hand, by Pappachi's "entomology," and on the other by Mammachi's "pickling."

In both Rushdie's *Midnight's Children* and Roy's *The God of Small Things*, pickling and pickle factories acquire a symbolic significance related as both are to discussions of history, time, and memory. In *Midnight's Children*, Rushdie uses pickling as a metaphor for his attempt to preserve in fiction the distinctiveness of Indian history. For his protagonist, Saleem, every pickle jar "contains, therefore, the most exalted of possibilities: the feasibility of the chutnification of history; the grand hope of the pickling of time" (p. 459). Pickling is Saleem's attempt to "immortalize" and as such his pickles are also tempered, colored, salted by the very moment of pickling. The opening chapter of Roy's novel, "Paradise Pickles & Preserves" plays on that earlier alignment of fiction/pickling as metaphors for the preservation or "chutnification" of history. Of course, "Paradise Pickles & Preserves" is the name that Chacko belatedly and with some family dissension attributes to Mammachi's large kitchen turned factory. The making of pickles has been Mammachi's strike for independence on the retirement of Pappachi, so it marks for a period her independent identity, but also marks in some way her contribution to the ideal of a self-sufficient independent India promoted in the Gandhi and Nehru years. As such its takeover by Chacko, and its subsequent decline suggests the failure of the post-Independence generation to capitalize on or carry through these ideals, a failure later epitomized by the wider political, economic, and cultural trauma inaugurated under Indira Gandhi's Emergency (1975–77).

Roy's archaeology, like Pappachi's entomology, is concerned with the order, classification, or categorization of things. "The bulk of the novel" after all, as Michael Gorra asserts, "defines a memory."

But this archaeology is also like Mammachi's pickling, an imprecise and ever evolving art. All are at times a matter of guesswork. Unlike Pappachi's entomology, however, Roy's archaeology, like Mammachi's pickling, offers us a rather different vision of what "History" (with a capital H) might be, how it might be written while attempting to upset conventional expectations of what constitutes the historical archive in the first place. For what we call "History," for Roy, should not be just the big public events like Independence, Partition, or Emergency but those more local, domestic, or intimate clashes of hope and fear, desire and loathing, that occur between individuals as well as communities and nations. Individual acts as much as the communal response to them, as *The God of Small Things* is keen to illustrate, shape history, and the trajectory of history. Histories are to be found in the ordinary moments or fragments, in the disorderly and discontinuous as well as in that orderly continuous narrative that we conventionally call "History."

Pappachi's entomology represents the prescriptions and limitations of this "History." As representative of the colonial order, he devotes his life to the factual narrative, the exactitudes of science and rationality. He "preserves" his moth in alcohol and searches for its fixed place in the history of evolution, an "account" that is destabilized and eclipsed over time. By contrast, Roy's archaeology of history, like Mammachi's pickling, eschews fixity. Her project is one of disturbance, movement, unearthing, dusting down, and reassembly of the fixed and received narrative of public or national events ("History") to bring to light the hidden or eclipsed histories therein. What Roy mounts then is no less than an excavation of "History" through the mobilization of "histories;" opening her narrative up to a plurality of voices, the many over the one, the small things (the bat baby, Kochu Thomban, the dead swallow in the skyblue Plymouth); what their place is and what they represent in the wider order. In *The God of Small Things*, Mammachi's pickling, metaphor for the attempt to record the many hidden "histories," is an imprecise art, never *fully* mastered as recorded by her leaking picklejars. Like Roy's hidden histories (which often conflict with or transgress received narratives or orders) Mammachi's pickles refuse to be classified; there is always confusion about whether they are actually jams or jellies. They seep out of the vessels that contain them when least expected: "Even now. . . . Paradise Pickles' bottles still leaked a little. It was imperceptible, but they did still leak, and on long journeys their labels became oily and transparent. The pickles themselves continued to be a little on the salty side" (p. 167).

Roy's archaeology is a form of excavation that can be said to be characteristic of the work of the postcolonial writer who returns to the historical archive precisely in order to disturb, to reclaim, rewrite, reinvent, and understand one's *emplacement* therein and it marks a wide body of writing from Margaret Atwood's *Surfacing* to Michael Ondaatje's *Anil's Ghost*. The Canadian writer and critic, Robert Kroetsch, for example, talking about his own attempts to understand the relations between this *emplacement* in the archive and the *particulars of place* that characterize his experience of Alberta in *Robert Kroetsch: Essays* (1983) argues:

It is a kind of archaeology that makes this place, with all its implications, available to us for literary purpose. We have not yet grasped the whole story; we have hints and guesses that slowly persuade us towards the recognition of larger patterns. Archaeology allows the fragmentary nature of the story, against the coerced unity of traditional history. Archaeology allows for discontinuity. It allows for layering. It allows for imaginative speculation. [. . . .] [E]ven the wrong-headed histories . . . become, rather than narratives of the past, archaeological deposits.

Here Kroetsch is talking not just about the nature of the postcolonial return to history but the form, structure, and style of writing it generates. The layered histories and sedimentations of the past un-earthed in Roy's text are replicated in the layered nature of her writing; short sentences, fragmented images, lives, memories, songs, rituals, traditions, piled up, one against the other, that are all part of a wider pattern or "deposit." Sometimes the connecting thread is thin, fragile, arbitrary, and used to highlight the very formality of the layering as with the sentence which links chapter one and two and with which Roy chooses to (re)start her story. That understand-ing of her project in *The God of Small Things* as a kind of archaeo-logical salvage is further developed by her characterization of the adult Rahel and Estha as "*frozen two-egg fossils*" suspended in the amber of childhood, "[t]*rapped in the bog* of a story that was and wasn't theirs" (p. 236, my italics). Roy's archaeology is an attempt then to return to that moment of seizure and suspension and to uncover the forces and tensions that activated it.

If Roy's archaeology can be understood as characteristic of the postcolonial project of liberating from the archive the many muffled voices therein, it can also be approached in terms of the wider questioning and incredulity towards the master narratives of "His-tory" or "Myth" prescient in postmodernism and the postmodernist return to history. Indeed, Roy's use as epigraph of a quotation from John Berger ("Never again will a single story be told as though it's the only one") directly focuses our attention on one of the important themes in the novel; the constructed and partial nature of all narra-tives that parade as or assume the authority of "History" and the necessity of finding a way to write in the differing perspectives and voices, the multiple histories. "History" like any other kind of nar-rative is a way of ordering the world and its events. Roy redoubles our attention on this human urge to make order, to find the pattern, while pointing out that the order(s) we create are just that; human constructs, ways of understanding the diverse elements that shape our own *placement* and *emplacement* in the world. For as Roy writes, in relation to the tragedy that befalls the Ipe family in that fateful fortnight in 1969, to suggest that "it all began when Sophie Mol came to Ayemenem *is only one way of looking at it*. Equally it could be argued that it actually began thousands of years ago. . . . That it really began in the days when the Love Laws were made. The laws that lay down who should be loved, and how" (p. 33, my italics). This questioning of historical perspective or point of view is one that Roy returns to again and again, in her narration of the action from multiple points of view, primarily through Rahel and Estha but also through the eyes of Ammu, Velutha, Vellya Paapen, and Baby Kochamma. It is another way of demonstrating the project of salvaging fragments. The redoubled focus on order and the ways in which it is punctured by the eruption of other orders is apparent in the structure or pattern that Roy, as author, rather self consciously imposes on the stories she wants to tell. The long opening chapter presenting a précis of events to come is followed by the orderly patterning of interweaving chapters. Past events are detailed in even numbered chapters and present events in odd-numbered ones, a "structure" which seems so regular that as Michael Gorra argues, "when Roy finally violates it, keeping her narration firmly in the past, the dissonance compels an extra degree of attention." So the rage for pattern or order (in historical narrative) and its disruption is reflected in the broken chain of Roy's narrative itself.

HISTORY HOUSES

Rahel and Estha's return to Ayemenem represents the postcolonial return to history and the historical archive. It is a return that simul-taneously reveals what is lost or hidden but which continues to haunt the historical archive, what is made visible again in the act of return — the tessellations of family. The aim of the return is a kind of exorcism of old ghosts, in order to facilitate new beginnings, new departures. It is then that most symbolic of returns in postcolonial writing, the return to history in order to learn from, break with or reinvent that past. Roy's novel does not follow the characteristic trajectory of the *bildungsroman*, or novel of childhood which tends to trace the formative conflicts which lead to the flight of the individual from the confines of family, community, and nation as represented in, for example, the figure of Stephen Dedalus in *A Portrait of the Artist as a Young Man* (1916), the work of one of Roy's favorite authors, James Joyce. It is rather an "anti-*bildungsroman*." Frozen in the past, Rahel and Estha have never really grown up. So by contrast, it opens not with the developments that inaugurate a leavetaking but the return to the moment of suspension. It traces what Leela Gandhi terms a "journey in re-verse — from the cosmopolitan wholeness of America to the quiet provincialism of Kerala" except that in Roy's Kerala of the 1990s, embedded in the transnational global trade in goods, services, and labor, these simple oppositions (cosmopolitanism vs. provincialism) are not as easily recognizable or distinguishable as Gandhi suggests.

The house that Rahel returns to is an emptied out shell of the past, full of the decaying and the decrepit, a *mausoleum* of dead, near dead, or never grown up, a house that is now a fitting twin for the haunted house of their childhood, "The History House." This first house, on the opposite side of the river Meenachal to their own, is a controlling image and suffused with its own symbolism. Once owned by the shadowy figure of Kairi Saipu, an Englishman "gone native," "Ayemenem's own Kurtz" (Roy's allusion here drawn from Joseph Conrad's *Heart of Darkness* [1902]), the History House now lies abandoned; its occupancy suspended by legal dispute. The History House functions to give voice to the double trauma of colonization. It is a recognition that the material organization and execution of the colonial project could and was also experienced as a trauma for the colonizing *as well as* the colonized culture. If Pappachi is a figure for the ambivalences that characterize the colonized, Kairi Saipu functions as a troubling figure for the colonizer who is in the process also suspended indefinitely between cultures, traditions, and identities. Roy's attention to the half remembered, half-told, and now disputed history of Kairi Saipu is an attempt to liberate the diverse allegiances and ambivalences from the singular story of colonialism. When Chacko explains to the twins the peculiar suspension between cultures and traditions that characterize the Ipes as "Anglophiles," as descendants of the old colonial elite, he figures them as a family "locked out" of "an old house at night. With all the lamps lit. And ancestors whispering inside." The children immediately suspect that Chacko's figurative house refers to a real one; to the ghost of Kairi Saipu and the "History House" across the river. In its state of suspended occupancy it offers a brief fugitive refuge to those other soon to be ghosts in the historical archive, Ammu and Velutha, whose story later refuses its own burial amid Baby Kochamma's lies and Chacko and Mammachi's complicity. They meet at the History House as lovers, and later when Estha, Rahel, and Sophie Mol attempt to flee there it becomes the site of another more traumatic and lifelong haunting; being the site of Velutha's violent death. Latterly its afterlife as "Heritage" or a repackaged "History" illustrates Roy's continuing interest in how the (colonial) past is managed, drained, repackaged, and appropriated in the name of global tourism (p. 126).

The house that Rahel returns to, and the relatives still living like Baby Kochamma, Kochu Maria, and even her beloved twin Estha, are united in stagnation in a moment of time. All are hostages. Their lives are held up or given over in ransom to someone else — Baby Kochamma to Father Mulligan, Kochu Maria to the Ipe family, and to the brother-in-law who arrives every fortnight to collect her meager wages and Estha, a walking ghost haunted by his indirect role in the death of Sophie Mol and Velutha. In this the Ipe family home betrays a stagnation characteristic of the Old Delhi of Anita Desai's *Clear Light of Day* (1980), itself described as "a great cemetery, every house a tomb. Nothing but sleeping graves. ... And here, here nothing happens at all. Whatever happened, happened long ago — in the time of the Tughlaqs, the Khiljis, the Sultanate, the Moghuls — that lot" (p. 5). Most particularly, it describes the family home of Desai's novel, a suffocating mausoleum of sorts, as if it "were the storeroom of some full, uninviting provincial museum" (p. 21). Of course, when Desai and Roy after her, suggest that these are the places where "nothing happens at all" they are really focusing on how these more intimate histories of conflict, desire, and rearrangement are denied a place and a relation to those recognized and linear arrangement of events in that which we conventionally call "History." For Desai and Roy, rather than being the place where *nothing* happens, these history houses are by contrast the sites where *everything* happens. For what happens in these more intimate spaces, in the family and the family home, in the working out of desire and conflict, love and hate, fear and hope, between individuals, between Ammu and Velutha, or between Rahel and Estha, colors the wider canvas.

If these decaying houses are, on the one hand, symbols of stagnation, of the outworn robes of the old colonial elite in the new India figured in both Desai's and Roy's novels, they are also the sites where regeneration and renewal is sought. As with Tara's return to Delhi in Desai's *Clear Light of Day*, Rahel returns to Ayemenem and the family house in order to understand and make peace with her past, to reclaim it and Estha after the separations and losses of childhood. This facilitates new moments of communion but also of separation between the twins. One such moment of communion, albeit painful, is their shared confrontation with the ghosts of the past in the kathakali performance that unfolds at the Ayemenem

Temple. There in the tales of Karna and Kunti, of Draupadi, Bhima, and Dushasana they are "joined" in a story. These stories have a living history in India. As Shashi Deshpande argues, "over the years they have been reinvested, reshaped, regionalised [but] living brothers are still a Ram-Lakshman, an ideal couple still a Ram-Sita or a Lakshmi-Narayan." So Estha and Rahel relive stories that mirror their own, stories of childhood separation, lost parents, the sacrifice of one child to save the other, stories in which the love laws are invoked to wreak vengeance in the face of imagined dishonor. As they both recognize on the floors of the Ayemenem temple, the "brutal extravagance" of Bhima's killing of Dushasana is "matched" across time by the "savage economy" of Velutha's death (p. 235). Here, the breach set up after the deaths of Sophie Mol and Velutha is temporarily bridged, they walk home together "He and She. We and Us"(p. 237). Beyond this compact no other consolation or healing is available to the twins for what haunts is loss (Sophie, Velutha, Ammu, childhood) and the impossibility of salvage. In a novel replete with "crossings," journeys across the boundaries of time, space and memory, the one "crossing" the twins cannot make is the recognition of their entrapment in a transgression not their own. They fail to realize that they are the "victims" not the "perpetrators." If they could, Roy argues, at least "fury" would have been an available mode of response, but "anger wasn't available to them" and they have nowhere to lay their grief and sense of responsibility: "There was nowhere to lay it down. It wasn't theirs to give away. It would have to be held. Carefully and for ever" (p. 191).

In the absence of anger, fury, a mode of redress, or of exorcism, they are condemned to repeat and in their repetition they broach an even greater taboo, incest, an act that speaks of their "hideous grief" rather than the "happiness" of being returned to one another and of the central theme of their betrayal by the family; the caretakers of the "Love Laws." What separates them in the first place, the "Love Laws" and the idea of *transgression* followed by the brutal betrayal of Mammachi and Baby Kochamma, is also what brings them back together. It is, however, another moment of defeat, of tragic loss, of hideous grief. In this Roy refuses any sense of easy ending. Rahel and Estha's refuge in each other, if it offers any release, is only the release of a kind of death like the death that stalks Ammu and Velutha in their moment of transgression, and identified in the last word of the novel "Tomorrow." What "Tomorrow" holds for Ammu and Velutha, as we know from early on in the novel, has already been ordained, decided, and narrated; what awaits Rahel and Estha is open to speculation but still held in suspension, frozen, rather as the twins have been since the death of Velutha and Sophie Mol.

CROSSING THE RIVER: INDIA AND THE WORLD

The Ipe family/house that Rahel and Estha return to is representative and at the same time at odds with the new Ayemenem in which it sits. If the Ipe family are dislocated, out of place, they are also absolutely *in place*, their troubled crossings of time and space rehearse the multiple crossings that characterizes India's past and present histories. Ayemenem of the early 1990s has both won and lost in its engagement with the new global economy. The transatlantic networks and movements of goods, money, and labor that once were at the heart of the British colonial enterprise continue despite the ostensible dismantling of Empire with Independence. The faces may have changed but as Roy argues, on a deeper level the structures that dictate India's engagement with the world have changed but slightly for those on the edge of the dominant order. If the Ayemenem of the early 1990s witnessed by Estha on his afternoon walks is one of "new, freshly baked, iced, Gulf-money houses built by nurses, masons, wirebenders and bank clerks who worked hard and unhappily in faraway places," that material success is compromised by other losses. For the occupants of Ayemenem, one of the losses incurred in their trading with the world is that the once mighty Meenachal, the lifeblood of the region, now "smells of shit, and pesticides bought with World Bank loans" (p. 13). Once supportive of an entire way of life, the river's place in the continuity of things has been disrupted. With the building of the saltwater barrage, the paddy-farmers can now reap two crops a year instead of one but the place of the Fisher People, the river's more ancient caretakers, has been usurped. As with Rushdie's focus in *Midnight's Children* on Mumbai's Koli fishermen as remnants of a primordial India, Ayemenem's Fisher People are the key to the region's many pasts that are being disrupted, erased, elided, and displaced in its troubled transactions with the managers of the global economy.

In this, Ayemenem is also India. It betrays something of the temper of the new and ongoing networks, histories, and rules of engagement that characterize India's post-Independence relations with the wider world. For Roy, India must be understood as a product of ancient *and* modern diaspora. Further, to understand Indian history and the sources of the conflicts that feed into the tragedies that befall the Ipe and Paapen families, the crucial role of the *multiple* conquests and crossings that make up diaspora must be acknowledged. In this, Roy's protagonists share much with those of a similar generation in Nayantara Sahgal's tale of life under Indira Gandhi's Emergency in *Rich Like Us* (1983) who are the "end result" of "many criss-crossing caravans, migrations and invading hordes" (p. 73).

In fact, the novel is all about crossings and crossing points, journeys started, made and derailed; the sum of all the departures from and returns to and across India that are traced in the many crossings that Pappachi, Chacko, Rahel, and her father make. Even those family members like Mammachi and Baby Kochamma who seem forever rooted in the Ayemenem house are marked by a complex history of cultural crossing and transaction, recorded, for example, in Baby Kochamma's ornamental garden. With its "lush maze of dwarf hedges, rocks, and gargoyles," its riotous varieties of Anthurium, beds of canna and phlox, marble cherub, "pink plaster of Paris gnome," twisting vines, bristling cacti, bonsai, rare orchids, and single blue lotus, Baby's garden stands as testament to the ways in which the Indian imagination is itself the product of a cross fertilization of cultures. Baby's garden is also Roy's rebuke to the troubled question of how to define India. In interview Roy asks: "How can one define India? There is no one language, there is no one culture. There is no one religion, there is no one way of life. There is absolutely no way one could draw a line around it and say, "This is India" or, "This is what it means to be Indian." Roy like Rushdie and Sahgal before her is arguing against the tyranny of the idea of a single pure culture that is identifiably or authentically Indian. By contrast she advocates the recognition of the inherent hybridity and plurality of the nation. In her particular focus on the Ipe family she gives voice to those who occupy the borders of what is seen as a predominantly Hindu India. As Nayantara Sahgal in her exacting essay "Some Thoughts on the Puzzle of Identity" argues:

To start conceiving of India as the cultural monopoly of Hindus, with every other culture on Indian soil seen as an imposter and outsider, would not only be a radical departure from the cardinal principles that went into the making of modern India, but a misrepresentation of Indian history and an abuse of cultural memory. It would result in a shrunken, artificial self-image made up of selected racial memories. It would deal the death-blow to my own cherished sense of Indianness, whose very essence is its ethnic and religious diversity, and its cultural plurality.(p.10)

Baby's Garden is testament then to the cultural *plurality* that both
Roy and Sahgal argue is crucial to any understanding of what it is
to be Indian. But by the time of Rahel's return to Ayemenem,
Baby's great project has been abandoned and her time and energies
are consumed by a new love; satellite TV, which unpacks the world
on India's doorstep in ways that are simultaneously alluring and
frightening, ways that seem to suggest that the heterogenous cultural
influences that had marked the garden have been replaced by a
more threatening and homogenous one. This is reiterated in the
programs both Baby Kochamma and Kochu Maria adore, *The Bold
and the Beautiful, Santa Barbara, Prime Bodies,* and *Wrestling Ma-
nia.* Whatever Baby's enchantment by the beautiful clothes and the
smart bitchy repartee of the American daytime soaps, her use of
satellite television as a way of "presiding" over and controlling her
engagement with the world is only partially successful for it also
rekindles her "old fears of Revolution and the Marxist-Leninist men-
ace" in the "growing numbers of desperate and dispossessed people," ethnic cleansing, famines, wars, and genocides it unpacks in
her living room (pp. 27–8).

In this Roy is drawing attention to ways in which India is shaped
by a global culture and it turn how it seeks to shape and understand
its place in that culture in local terms. The relations between what
is home and what is the world demand reconfiguration in the face
of expanding global networks and systems of communications,
which bring the world closer in ways Baby cannot always control.
Globalization begets new kinds of negotiation of space and place
and it demands new kinds of mapping. In her attention to Baby's
own troubled negotiations with the world, Roy explores India's own
understanding of itself as an inevitably and already hybridized culture subject to new and ongoing transactions with the world which
work as pervasively on it as the "communist patcha" in Baby's
garden to either gloss or elide the variety of cultural influences that

make up the nation. Roy is also trying to illustrate in her examination of the repackaging of kathakali, for example, the role of India as sending *as well as* receiving culture in these transactions. In this, we must also remain alert to the ways in which *The God of Small Things* is itself a part of this matrix—it sends a particular vision of India and Indian history out into the world and is part of a wider transnational cultural economy that shapes the way in which the world approaches and understands India as much as it reflects upon the ways in which the world outside has shaped and continues to shape India.

CASTE

If *The God of Small Things* seeks to revisit the ways in which colonization disrupted the systems, structures, knowledge, values, and beliefs which underpinned how Indians understood their space and place in the world, it also seeks to interrogate the other face of colonization: what it fails to change, i.e. how certain structures and systems survived the experience of colonization. It works to uncover the ways in which colonialism often incorporated rather than disturbed native hierarchies like that represented by caste. The arrival of Christianity, for example, did little to fundamentally change the workings of the caste system. Though caste was originally present only in Hinduism, Syrian Christians of Mammachi's and Baby Kochamma's class are in effect what Roy terms "Caste Christians sharing their Hindu neighbours revulsion at Untouchability." The attempts made by Untouchables (among them Velutha's grandfather, Kelan) to escape the indignities of Untouchability, with the arrival of a new political order are unsuccessful. They convert to the prevailing religion of the colonizers, Christianity, in the hope that a change in status and experience will follow.

But as practised by the British, colonialism and the Independence that follows it compounds rather than corrects the material, social, and cultural dispossession of Untouchables:

[Under the British] they were made to have separate churches, with separate services, and separate priests. . . . After Independence they found they were not entitled to any Government benefits like job reservations or bank loans at low interest rate, because officially, on paper, they were Christians, and therefore casteless. It was a little like having to sweep away your footprints without a broom, Or worse, not being *allowed* to leave footprints at all. (p. 74)

A similar fate awaits Velutha, the only card holding member of the Marxist Party almost a century later. Resented by the other Touchable workers for "ancient reasons of their own," it is clear that Marxism like Christianity fails to substantially overhaul the caste system. Even Chacko in his ideological spats with Comrade Pillai recognizes that Pillai's cries "(Caste is Class, comrades)" are "pharisaic" (p. 281); empty promises. The boundaries of caste are rigorously controlled and policed before, during, and after British occupation, as Velutha and Ammu find out to both their own and the twins cost. Both knowingly step outside the "love laws," the boundaries of the caste system. Velutha, as a Paravan the lowest of the Untouchables does so in becoming a carpenter and in his relationship with Ammu, while she knowingly does so in first marrying and then divorcing a Hindu outsider and then by falling in love with Velutha. As Roy concedes in interview with Maya Jaggi, both are joined in transgression, they "are external to their communities, outcasts to their castes." While Ammu and Velutha are separated by caste, Roy argues that their relationship and the responses to it if they are culturally specific are also emblematic of a universal "human nature": "[H]uman society has [always] found ways in which to divide itself, to make war across these divisions, to make love across these divisions. [My book is] really a way of seeing, a way of presenting the irreconcilable sides of our nature, our ability to love so deeply yet be so brutal."

Such is the internalization of the divides of caste that it is Velutha's father, Vellya Paapen, torn between fear and duty who enlightens Mammachi to the details of the lovers' offenses. He thereby furthers the novel's central theme of betrayal — of children by parents, of family by community. His betrayal occasions others, that of Velutha by his would be Marxist colleagues and the community more generally and of Ammu by family, community, and nation. Mammachi's first response to the news is to lock Ammu in her bedroom, an imprisonment that functions as a metaphor for Ammu's wider entrapment within the inherited caste values and boundaries of others. This imprisonment arguably leads to the death of Sophie Mol and Velutha, mirrored by Ammu's death in the hotel room of the Alleppey Bharat Lodge, itself reiterated in the death of the sparrow in the back of the decrepit sky blue Plymouth years later. By contrast, however, for Velutha the full "Terror" of his transgression is "unspooled" (p. 257) in a single night in the grounds of the History House.

FORM, ARCHITECTURE, AND KATHAKALI

Much critical attention has focused on the form and structure of *The God of Small Things*. In interview with Taisha Abraham, Roy attests to the critical relationship between the novel's design and its coherence: "It was really a search for coherence — design coherence — in the way that every last detail of a building — its doors and windows, its structural components — have, or at least ought to have, an aesthetic, stylistic integrity, a clear indication that they belong to each other, as must a book, I didn't just write my book. I designed it." If design coherence is critical so also is the relationship between form and content, between how a story is narrated and what is being narrated for the way a story reveals itself is as important for Roy as the story itself. In her WordsWorth interview Roy attests:

The way the story is told, or the structure of the book, tells you a different story [than one about doomed love or illusory happiness]. The structure of the book ambushes the story—by that I mean the novel ends more or less in the middle of the story and it ends with Ammu and Velutha making love and it ends on the word tomorrow. Though you know that what tomorrow brings is terrible it is saying that the fact that this [relationship between Ammu and Velutha] happened at all is wonderful. I don't think I offer you one thing.

Indeed, Roy does not offer just one way of thinking about form and architecture. Crucial to an understanding of the novel's architecture are the structures that dominate and organize that other great instrument of storytelling excavated in *The God of Small Things*, kathakali.

Originating in the seventeenth century and native to Kerala, this highly stylized dance-drama is based on the representation of classical stories from the great Indian epics (the *Mahabaratha* and the *Ramayana*) and the *puranas*; the diverse collection of wisdom and stories which are the bibles of popular Hinduism. It is important to note that for the local spectator the tales are predominantly *familiar* ones, overwhelmingly stories that the spectator already knows in some form or substance. This sense of being mesmerized by the performances of stories one already knows becomes the basis for the construction of *The God of Small Things*. Strategically, Roy tries to give her readers that sense of entering a story that they *already* know, which is partly why the long first chapter provides a précis of events to come. She mobilizes the open-ended structures of narration characteristic of *kathakali* in the overall design of the novel, the allure of which she vividly paints in the description of Rahel and Estha's experience in their visit to the Ayemenem temple:

It didn't matter that the story had begun, because kathakali discovered long ago that the secret of the Great stories is that they *have* no secrets. The Great Stories are the ones you have heard and want to hear again. The ones you can enter anywhere and can inhabit comfortably. They don't deceive you with thrills and trick endings. They don't surprise you with the unforeseen. They are as familiar as the house you live in. Or the smell of your lover's skin. You know how they end, yet you listen as though you don't. In the way that although you know that one day you will die, you live as though you won't. In the Great Stories you know who lives, who dies, who finds love, who doesn't. And yet you want to know again. *That* is their mystery and their magic. (p. 229)

Roy's description is really a metafictional moment, where she offers a commentary on her own fiction making, on the architecture of her own story. For the appeal of kathakali is also that of Roy's story; it can "fly you across whole worlds in minutes" or "stop for hours to examine a wilting leaf." The author, like the actor/dancer, defies linearity, manipulates chronology, and escapes the restrictions of clock time.

Historically, *kathakali* functioned mainly in the palaces of rajas and kings, but today has a much expanded and often non-Malayali audience as noted in *The God of Small Things*. Here, Roy details its mutilation in the shorter tailored packages demanded by the tourist hotels. Simultaneously, however, she also narrates the increasingly desperate attempt to exorcise that "humiliation in the Heart of Darkness" in the ritualistic performances designed by the *kathakali* men "to ask pardon" for "corrupting" the Gods' "stories" (p. 229). Traditionally performed by an all male company each kathakali actor-dancer plays a variety of roles, easily identifiable to a Malayali audience as specific character types through the deployment of codified make-ups and elaborate and colorful costumes. As Phillip Zarilli documents, the actor-dancers create their roles by using a repertory of dance steps, choreographed patterns of stage movement, and an intricate and complex language of hand gestures for literally speaking their character's dialogue with their hands (*mudras*) as well as using particular face and eye movements to express the internal states (*bhasu*) of each character. For Roy, the actor-dancer's "body *is* his soul," "planed and polished, pared down, harnessed wholly to the task of storytelling" (p. 230). Just as the characters of kathakali are identifiable to the audience through their codified make-up and elaborate clothing, in emulating the structures of kathakali in the design of her novel, Roy establishes and identifies her characters to her readers through the deployment of a series of codified images, tropes, and symbols. Rahel, for example, is identified by her "fountain in a Love-in-Tokyo," Bata sandals, her toy wristwatch with the time painted on it, her yellow-rimmed red plastic sunglasses which paint the world an "angry red," and not least by Pappachi's moth and its "unusually dense dorsal tufts" which spreads its shadowy wings over her heart. Estha, in turn is identifiable by his beige and pointy shoes ("from where the angry feelings rose"), Elvis puff, pointed collars, drainpipe trousers, Wisdom Exercise Notebooks, and the characteristic refrain from the cartoon "Popeye" ("dum dum"). Further, Estha and Rahel are united by their mobilization of language games, on public and private levels. These take on heightened significance in moments of crisis and indicate to the reader something of the internal state (*bhasu*) of their character(s). Equally, just as the all-male tradition of actor-dancers in *kathakali* demands that men play the roles of women, indeed, one of the actor-dancers in the Ayemenem temple assumes an indeterminate gendered identity his body grown "soft and womanly, a man with breasts, from doing female parts for years" (p. 232), so both men and women in Roy's novel refuse bounded gendered identities and the set roles or authority that go with them.

Estha and Chacko are pertinent examples. Estha's blurred gender identity is suggested on numerous occasions. First, by his twin status, followed up in the chapter titled "Mrs. Pillai, Mrs. Eapan, Mrs. Rajagopalan" in which all three children dress up as Hindu ladies complete with saris and bindis but where Estha is the acknowledged "draping expert." This playful feminization of Estha can be contrasted with the more traumatic one enacted in his assault at the Abhilash Talkies. There he is pictured as a junior Julie Andrews with a "nun's voice, as clear as clean water," this is set against his assailant's "gravelley" voice, an opposition further developed in Roy's narration of the assault itself. Estha's response is marked by a retreat into invisibility and silence, so that he is Estha Alone, Estha the Quiet. The troubled outcome of this attack is still further retreat, dramatized in the descriptions of his afterlife in his father's house where he refuses both the traditional privileges of masculinity and the public life of men and takes on a role not unlike that of Kochu Maria, of family servant, much to the initial embarrassment of his father and stepmother. By the time of Rahel's return, Estha is a ghostly figure whose presence barely registers.

Similarly, and as if mirroring Chacko and Estha's emasculation, Ammu and Rahel confound inherited models of femininity. Having married outside her community, she leaves and subsequently divorces her husband. She initiates an affair across caste boundaries with Velutha in which she is the sexual teacher. Rahel's progressin the world is marked by an equal subversion of gender categories. While Estha mimics Julie Andrews, she aligns herself with Christopher Plummer, *The Sound of Music's* Captain von Trapp. Because of her general refusal to conform at school her teachers blacklist her for her incendiary actions. It is, they conclude, "*as*

though she didn't know how to be a girl" (p. 17). In fact, the unor-
thodox nature of the Ipe family structure means that Rahel grows
up like her mother before her with "No Locusts Stand I." This
creates a vacuum in which Rahel is isolated and marginalized but
at the same time somewhat free to continue her investigations into
"life and how it ought to be lived."

The intricate interplay of elements (acting, dancing, gesture,
percussion, vocals, costume, makeup) and the highly codified and
choreographed nature of kathakali performances provides further
basis for the analogy that can be drawn between the design of
kathakali and that of Roy's novel with its interplay of elements
(form, style, character, languages, landscape, use of time) and its
intimate, interconnecting and highly intricate patterns of repetition.
Repetition, as strategy for keeping the story "on track" is, Roy suggests, fundamental to the illumination of the novel's greater themes,
how the "smallest things connect to the biggest things, every detail
of childhood, even the light on water, connects to history and
politics and geological time." These repetitions are both various and
numerous; they can be of a key phrase, word or idea ("Lay Ter,"
"Things can change in a day," "Not together, but almost") or of
events or moments that recur in different shapes or form. In this
respect we could compare, for example, the description of the death
of Ammu in the grimy hotel room of the Bharat Lodge in Alleppey
(pp. 161-2), and the death of the female sparrow years later in the
now decrepit sky blue Plymouth (p. 296). As Roy concedes repetition is crucial in "reassuring the reader that he or she is in good
hands. Repeated words and phrases have a rocking feeling, like a
lullaby. They help take away the shock of the plot—death, lives
destroyed or the horror of the settings—a crazy, chaotic, emotional
house, the sinister movie theatre." That is why in part the novel is
replete with repetitions, echoes, and reminders.

Roy herself suggests the analogy of laying down a music track to describe the choreographic interplay of elements in the novel. "It was," she argues "like continuously adding more instruments, making it richer." For Cynthia Vanden Dreisen the novel is composed of "Fugues" in which "one movement is counterpointed against another [with] motifs, phrases, images flowing across, counterpointing, refracting, intertwining with each other." While the intricate codification, the repertory of steps and choreography are important in kathakali, one of its other primary characteristics as a system of cultural performance is its versatility and flexibility; each production, translation, or adaptation offers to both its participants and spectators not just an inherited set of conventional expectations and associations but also the opportunity to manipulate these features to fashion novel performances which turn that performance into something else (for both participants and spectators). The performance witnessed by Rahel and Estha can be read as a typical example of how kathakali, the representation of the classical and popular stories which constitute a general or collective cultural archive, once *replayed* can become a vehicle for the performance and interpretation of more local and private histories. The desperate display on the floors of the temple represents an attempt by the performers to rise above their abasement and retreat into the majesty of a past tradition. This has both positive and negative aspects. The security of entering a past tradition in which the story is the "safety net," offers the performer "shape" and "structure" and allows him not only to gather up the shreds of an outworn identity but also the power to reconnect the basic forces of life: "His Love. His Madness. His Hope" (p. 231). However, Roy's kathakali actors are struggling to adapt to a changing world and the retreat into tradition while it offers a space for the expression of their despair at the transformation of their art into just another commodity in the market, in the end this can do little to change the material realities of their lives. What is a safety valve can also be a dangerous prison as Roy reiterates:

Ironically, his struggle is the reverse of an actor's struggle — he strives not to *enter* a part but to escape it. But this is what he cannot do. In his abject defeat lies his supreme triumph. He *is* Karna, whom the world has abandoned. Karna Alone. Condemned goods. A prince raised in poverty. [...] Majestic in his complete despair. Praying on the banks of the Ganga. Stoned out of his skull. (p. 232)

Here Roy is also alluding to the dangers of mythic models — how they can be a force of containment as well as liberation. Typical are those inherited models of Indian womanhood that continue to shape women's space and place in Indian culture. As Shashi Deshpande elaborates, "to be as pure as Sita, as loyal as Draupadi, as beautiful as Lakshmi . . . as strong as Durga — these are all the ultimate role models we cannot entirely dismiss." If both the kathakali dancers and Roy's twin protagonists find in the replaying of myth new understandings of self, Roy herself extends this refashioning of a base set of rules to produce a novel performance in her negotiation of a non-standard English in the novel. For standard English is made up of a base set of rules which operate around an inherited set of conventional expectations and associations which both Roy and her twin protagonists refashion precisely in order to first dislocate and then resituate those inherited expectations and associations.

Inherent to *kathakali* are what Phillip Zarilli describes as macrostructural narratives. These are the stories that are used to sum up a whole scene or even a whole play like, for example, the story of the triumph of good over evil that could be represented by, for example, a battle in which a figure embodying evil is killed by a figure embodying divine righteousness. One could argue that the exploration of these perennial themes (like the triumph of love over loss or joy over sorrow) is the macrostructural frame on which *The God of Small Things* hangs. The success of Roy's novel remains its open-ended nature. Depending on how you read the novel, you could conclude that the perennial theme is the defeat of caste divisions by love as represented by the relationship between Ammu and Velutha or, conversely, the defeat of love by the machinations of the caste system as illustrated by the murder of Velutha and the symbolic passing of responsibility for this onto the shoulders of Estha and Rahel by Baby Kochamma.

LANGUAGE AND INTERTEXTS

One of the first stories that Rahel and Estha remember is Shakespeare's *The Tempest* as found in Lamb's *Tales from Shakespeare*, essentially short prose versions of the plays written for children. Language carries culture and it carries history. In the context of Empire, the English language functioned as a vehicle for the transmission of a matrix of cultural beliefs, values and ideologies; stories like Shakespeare's *The Tempest* and Kipling's *The Jungle Book* were integral to the ideological wing or "civilising mission" of British imperialism as propagated by Thomas Macaulay, for instance, in which an education in English was promulgated as the prerequisite to the formation of an Indian ruling elite. In Shakespeare's *The Tempest*, one of the primary conflicts explored is that between the ruler, Prospero, and the ruled, Caliban. The latter articulates concisely the dilemma of the colonized induced to take on a new language: "You taught me language; and my profit on't/ Is, I know how to curse." For Caliban, the advantage of this new language is that it allows him to express and represent his own condition in ways that are recognizable as powerful to both colonizer and colonized. Roy, too, draws on this idea of language as a powerful and subversive tool for the colonized *as well as* the colonizer in *The God of Small Things* in her particular focus on language, specifically in how she renders an indigenous Indian-English and in demonstrating how her twin protagonists renegotiate their space and place in the world through the deployment of language games.

"Language," says Roy "is the skin on my thought." Consistently in reviews the issue of Roy's innovative deployment of non-standard or indigenous Indian English has been applauded for its ability to portray the world as if "new minted." Standard English is rendered alien and unfamiliar. Cynthia Vanden Dreisen's essay in *Arundhati Roy: The Novelist Extraordinary* (1998) notes the resemblances between Roy's devices for making the language strange and those strategies of "abrogation" and "appropriation" through which the postcolonial writer more generally attempts to interrogate and remake the language of the colonizer. These strategies are more fully delineated in Bill Ashcroft et al., *The Empire Writes Back: Theory and Practice in Post-Colonial Literatures* (1989). In Ashcroft et al., abrogation and appropriation are related processes. Abrogation encompasses "a refusal of the categories of the imperial culture, its aesthetic, its illusory standard of normative or 'correct' usage" together with the usurpation of assumptions of traditional and fixed meanings. Roy's dismembering of standard English can be read in these terms. She constantly breaks the conventional rules of grammar and syntax, abandons standard punctuation, reworks capitals, coins neologisms, imports typographical devices, litters her text with anagrams, puns, acrostics, and palindromes (*Malayalam, Madam I'm Adam*). In rendering Estha and Rahel's attempt to understand and assert their place in the world through language, she has telescoped words together (suddenshudder, furrywhirring, sariflapping, slipperoily), exchanged syllables between them (redly dead), read words backwards (*nataS in their seys*), split them apart (Lay Ter, Bar Nowl) and coined in the process new words (hostling, stoppited, bursty).

Concomitant with the dissection of English outlined above is

Roy's mobilization of strategies of appropriation, which work to make the language speak for the local context and experience and to bring it under the influence of the vernacular tongue and what Ashcroft et al. describe as "the complex of speech habits which characterise the local language." We can see this in the telescoping processes outlined above but also in Roy's dispersal of Malayalam words in her text for these have an important function in inscribing locality and difference. When *The God of Small Things* was published in the United States, Roy was asked to provide a glossary or rework some of the Malayalam words. This she refused to do on the basis that the non-Malayalam or non-Indian reader be forced into what Ashcroft et al. term "an active engagement with the horizons of the culture in which these terms have meaning." Some critics, like Mary Condé, are less convinced by Roy's rebuttals of the requirements to translate and point to evidence of internal glossing or explanation like the translations of "Ammu," "Baba," "Mon," and "Mol," designed to make the reading process easier for the non-Malayalam reader. These can have the effect of reinscribing the authority of the translated word and elevating rather than challenging the receptor culture generally. Bearing in mind Condé's qualifications, it is, I think, still possible to argue that Roy's linguistic strategies offer a ground plan for the expression of an Indian-English that displays both its hybridized cultural inheritance and the gains and losses that mark it. David Punter illuminates these losses in his *Postcolonial Imaginings* (2000) when he argues that "the language used to recount the story is haunted by the languages in which the protagonists might have told the tale — had they their own language, or indeed in this case *any* language, at their disposal." While he recognizes the losses that striate Roy's languages, he fails to recognize the small ways in which the novel's protagonists *do* manage to refashion language to speak back, however incompletely they do this. Dreisen, for example, sees the twins' deployment of language games, particularly their reading backwards as "a powerful subversion of the established order: they read the word as they read the world in oppositional mode to that ordained by the powers that be." The children assert their presence through language; they refuse the invisibility attached to inherited scripts, an "effrontery" practiced by and learned in the first instance from Ammu and encouraged by Velutha. They revel not just in the exuberance of the word but the wor(l)d turned upside down. We can see this in their marvel at the simplicity of words like "cuff links" and their celebratory dismembering of a world like "Nictitating" (p. 189) which reduces language to a kind of nonsense; itself an assertion of power and of mastery over the word.

But if Roy seizes on Caliban's speaking back as a model for how her twins articulate the particularities of their own emplacement in the world and speak back to those in power, she is also keen to recognize the ways in which that new language, English, opened and continues to open India and Indians to the world in new, exciting, and liberating ways. As experienced through the medium of an education in English literature, English also offered Indians new kinds of identification, new lenses from which to view themselves but also the world and their place in it. While speaking of the losses incurred with the imposition of English, Shashi Deshpande also speaks eloquently of the new perspectives afforded in the process: "Yet I never can forget that the Empire was for me the bridge to an enchanted world, one which opened up for me as soon as I read a book that began: 'It is a truth universally acknowledged that a single man in possession of a good fortune, must be in want of a wife.'" The evidence of English literature as the bridge to an enchanted as well as a bittersweet world is everywhere apparent in *The God of Small Things*. We see it in the children's love of Kipling, Baby's attachment to Shakespeare, and the children's particular rendition of scenes from *The Tempest* and *Julius Caesar*, the allusions to Conrad's *Heart of Darkness*, Chacko's melodramatic quotations from *The Great Gatsby*, in Comrade Pillai's exaggerated pride in his daughter, Latha's, recitation of Walter Scott's "Lochinvar," and Lenin's breathless, fluent but bewildered recitation of Mark Anthony's "Friends, Romans, Countrymen" speech from *Julius Caesar*. Together with a variety of other overt and covert high and popular cultural intertexts like *The Sound of Music*, *Meet Me in St. Louis*, *The Bronze Buckaroo*, *Modern Times*, and *Mutiny on the Bounty* and the range of Indian stories, myths, and folksongs interspersed in the text—Roy details the ongoing cross-fertilization central to Indian culture across the ages. These texts in themselves often offer new ways of thinking the story Roy herself tells. Mary Condé, suggests, for example, that "the allusions to *Gatsby* and *Julius Caesar* reinforce the novel's central theme of betrayal, whereas *The Sound of Music* and 'Lochinvar' constitute in themselves betrayals, offering as they do utterly misleading stories of beleaguered lovers who end happily together." Roy's intertextuality continues to illustrate the ways in which texts travel across cultures; implicated in and part of a wider political economy and system of exchange. In this, *The God of Small Things* and the tradition of Indo-Anglian fiction of which it is a part is no exception.

3

The Novel's Reception

The *God of Small Things* has enjoyed wide success with reviewers and the reading public alike and it has launched Arundhati Roy on the world stage in ways that few could have predicted but many have been quick to analyze. To understand the scale of its success and the breadth of its critical reception we have first to recognize its status and achievement as a first novel. When it appeared in Britain in April 1997 (after its launch in Delhi), the novel was duly praised by critics such as Michael Gorra, Shirley Chew, Ian Jack, and a diverse gathering of fellow novelists like John Updike, Salman Rushdie, Ali Smith, and Meera Syal. "A gripping tale of love and loss" proclaimed Uttara Choudhury in the *Financial Times* while the *Economist* pointed to a "quite astonishing first novel by any standards — broad in its historical sweep, emotionally profound and marvellously acute and delicate." For Michael Gorra in the *London Review of Books*, Roy's novel is "original," a "rarity in post-colonial fiction, a largely-conceived and ambitious book about private life" while Shirley Chew in the *Times Literary Supplement* remarks on how "Roy's finest touches spring from her skill at registering the unsayable terrors lodged below the surface of everyday

things." Chew continues by noting the "fidelity to detail; the adroit-
ness and imagination with which human motives and behaviour are
handled in the novel." Similarly, for Boyd Tonkin in *The Independent*, Roy's novel is an "ancient drama played out against an unmis-
takably modern backdrop" which turns "the clash of tongues and
histories in Kerala into the motor of its comedy, its lyricism and its
fine intelligence." It was perhaps of little surprise then that the
novel won the Booker Prize in October 1997, passing at the post
contributions by Jim Crace, Bernard MacLaverty, Madeleine St.
John, Tim Parks and the other newcomer Mick Jackson. It featured
heavily on authors and critics lists for "Books of the Year" including
that of Shusha Guppy who heralded the arrival of an "authentic
new voice." Will Hutton in more measured tones cherished its
"refreshing originality" while William Dalrymple in *The Sunday
Times* fueled the already well-oiled publicity machine in proclaim-
ing it "the great soaring masterpiece of 1997."

In India, the critical reception of the novel has been such that
Roy's ongoing engagement with the matrix of private and public
history and mores has led to both controversy and acclaim. Sunil
Sethi in *Outlook*, suggests that Roy's novel is "well-paced, evocative
and densely-plotted" while for Supriya Chaudhuri in the *Asian Age*,
"Roy handles the shifting surfaces of past and present with extraordinary fineness and delicacy, producing a controlled, intricate narrative structure through which the themes of love, spite, betrayal,
hatred and guilt run like a spider's web." It was also widely wel-
comed by a host of Indo-Anglian writers like Kamala Das, Anita
Desai, Amitav Ghosh, and with some reservations by Nayantara
Sahgal. Despite the general acclaim and interest in the novel and,
more overtly, the novelist, controversy raged in Indian circles. It was
criticized by left-wing Indian critics and Marxists who took issue
with Roy's representation and alleged denigration of the communist
leader, E.M.S. Namboodiripad, and by right-wing elements of the

press who also objected to what was seen as the novel's overly revealing portrayal of cross-caste relationships and community responses to them. Controversy was such that criminal proceedings were filed against Roy, under Section 292 of the Indian Penal code, on the charge of corrupting public morality by a lawyer from Kerala, Sabu Thomas. Roy herself has responded to criticisms of the novel in India by drawing attention to the ways in which writing about and cultural representations of India are policed on a national level by what she calls the "Proper Light Brigade": "If you write about Brahmins or kathakali dancers, you're writing for the West. If you mention *The Sound of Music*, you have betrayed Indian culture. India is a country that lives in several centuries, and some of the centuries have not been at all pleased with my book. But I say replace ethnic purity and 'authenticity' with honesty."

In America, critical reception mirrored the British acclaim. Alice Truax writing for *The New York Times Book Review* praised Roy's "anti-*bildungsroman*" for its ambitious attempt to retrieve the complexity of lost histories, seeing in the novel's elaborate and circuitous reconstruction of past events "both a treasure hunt (for the story itself) and a court of appeals (perhaps all the witnesses were not heard; perhaps all the evidence was not considered." In a similar vein, Rosemary Dinnage in *The New York Review* sees Roy's mapping of the Indian South—tropical, Marxist Kerala—as an important counterbalancing gesture to the palimpsest of the Indian north and the great cities of Delhi, Mumbai, and Calcutta collectively generated by fellow Indo-Anglian writers like Salman Rushdie, Amit Chaudhuri, Nayantara Sahgal, and Vikram Chandra. Indian and British reviews, notably Maya Jaggi's articles on Roy in *The Guardian* and *The Irish Times* had already overtly focused on the narrative of the "discovery" of Roy and the fairy-tale nature of her signing up by her agent, David Godwin. The sedimentation of this narrative of Roy's rise to prominence in the American critical reviews and interviews is matched only by the obsessive desire to conflate Roy the author with the protagonists of her novel. Dinnage's review is just one of many that cannot help but obsessively add to the mythmaking process: "[E]veryone will have heard by now that she is beautiful, bohemian, [and] wrote in secret for four years." She concludes that Roy herself may be "the goddess of small things."

If there was controversy in India over the content of Roy's novel, there were also some important qualifying critiques of the novel in Britain and America. Shirley Chew's review in forgiving tones notes that "its weaknesses are the kind one might expect in a first novel: the most obvious being a tendency to overwrite." For Chew, typical of these weaknesses is Roy's overuse of symbols, which are "repeated and repeatedly underlined—Pappachi's moth, the house of the 'Black Sahib' across the river, Ammu's tangerine-coloured transistor." Michael Gorra continues this critique of Roy's style, which he considers overly "pawed" by Rushdie's: "She is too fond of symbols, similes, alliteration, capital letters and the pathetic fallacy." Moreover, for Gorra, Roy like Rushdie displays a tendency to "over interpret her characters" adding that Rushdie "gets away with it because he's fundamentally a comic writer. Roy is not." Michiko Kakutani in *The New York Times* and Eileen Battersby in *The Irish Times* also focus overtly on Roy's drawing of character, with the latter dismissively reiterating over a series of reviews her criticism that Roy "seems to believe that characterisation begins and ends with physical description" while Kakutani concludes that Roy is "sometimes overzealous in foreshadowing her characters fate resorting on occasion to darkly portentous clues." Where Dinnage finds Roy's use of flashback subtle and warranting of close attention, for Battersby, Roy's "convoluted" and "laboured" narrative strategies are problematic and "unconvincing," with the "shifts of time" operating as little more than "impressionistic flashbacks." Gorra is also somewhat unconvinced by Roy's narrative strategies, particularly her deployment of the child's eye view, which he understands as compromised by a failure "to maintain a consistent point of view" and a tendency to adopt a "faux-naif style even when she's not looking through their eyes" which leads him to conclude that the "social analysis" offered often "jars with the childlike tone." Concomitant with this elaboration on the limitations of Roy's style has been the attention directed at Roy's pushing of the boundaries of genre. Again Battersby seems somewhat wrong-footed by the novel's movement between genres; tragedy, melodrama, "popular romance, the grotesque," and what she terms "a crypto magic realism" while Peter Kemp in *The Sunday Times* is equally phlegmatic about Roy's deployment of "magic realism as recycled candyfloss." One could argue that both critiques are lacking in any real definition of what they understand by magic realism and what models they take as normative. The question of perspective is all, and Roy is adamant that she is not writing magic realism, that realism rather than magic realism frames her project in *The God of Small Things*. Elleke Boehmer's summation of Roy's liberties with realism as an "extravagant realism" in her inquisitive essay "East is East and South is South: The Cases of Sarojini Naidu and Arundhati Roy" (*Woman: A cultural review*, 2000), seems rather closer in vein to Roy's views on the organizational principle of her novel than that offered by Kemp or Battersby.

A predominant feature of the marketing and critical reception of Roy's novel and, indeed, of Roy herself, has been the issue of exoticism and the exotic. Dinnage partly recognizes the ways in which as a Western reader she is conditioned historically to respond to "the rich and (to us) exotic, setting" of the novel. But while she reiterates Roy's rebuke that "she is not marketing fairyland," she fails in her review to really question or problematize that conditioning or to consider how that category of the Indian exotic might itself be a Western construct. Rather, and in spite of Roy's assertions, she continues by providing a revealing list that continues to install and maintain "India" as "exotica" for the Western imagination. In a similar fashion, writing for *The Australian*, Beth Yahp praises the novel for its "tantalising mix of Indian exotica, mysticism and history on a domestic and national level" but never really attempts to understand or question both her decidedly uncritical deployment of these terms and the variety of Roy's *uses* of the exotic. Equally and more problematically, Battersby's reviews, with little real elaboration on the evidence for such a view, consistently dismisses the novel as little more than "an exercise in designer exotica." Neither Dinnage, Yahp, or Battersby move from a recognition of the presence of the exotic to a critique of either their own or Roy's deployment of exoticism per se. By contrast, Graham Huggan in what is an entertaining and energized dissection of the making and marketing of Indo-Anglian fiction in the West in *The Post-Colonial Exotic-Marketing the Margins* (2001), aligns Roy's work with that of Salman Rushdie and Vikram Seth in its mobilization of a "knowing" exoticism. For Huggan, Roy's novel rather than merely replicating India as the site for the fulfillment of western categories of the East as exotic, as has been suggested in reviews like Battersby's, mobilizes instead what he terms a "strategic" exoticism. This is evident in how the novel "displays" and "ironises its own lushly romantic images, its metaphor-laden language, its transferred Conradian primitivist myths." In Huggan's understanding, Roy's work is overtly conscious of "the recent history of Indo-Anglian fiction, and of the parallel history of imperialist nostalgia in the West: the films of [David] Lean and Merchant and Ivory; the profitable *Heart of Darkness* industry; the travel writing business with its recuperative parodies of imperial heroism and derring-do." Always provocative, he goes on to argue that Roy's attention to the trade, commerce, and currency of nostalgic images in *The God of Small Things* is political, designed "to trap the unwary reader into complicity with the Orientalisms of which the novel so hauntingly relates" while also being in part a kind of "meta-exoticism," a text obsessively "reveal[ing] the link between the perceptual mechanism of the exotic and the metropolitan marketing of Indian literature in English in the West."

Moving from the analysis of Roy's mobilization of a strategic exoticism in the novel, Boehmer's essay noted earlier focuses on how the critical construction and reception of Roy as an Indian woman writer illustrates a series of troubling parallels and continuities between her reception and promotion, "much hyped and hailed as the long awaited female Rushdie," and the remarkable fate of the Indian woman poet, Sarojini Naidu in London in the 1890s. Alongside what has already been noted as the obsession with the narrative of Roy's discovery and rise to fame, for Boehmer, what has been prominent in the critical reception of Roy is "her being female in a group of predominantly male younger Indian novelists . . . and related to this, her intensely feminine elfin beauty." For Boehmer, the construction in the critical reception of Roy of a "contemporary Indian literary femininity" when compared with the fate of Naidu in the 1890s has much to tell us "about how the West continues to read the East, setting it up as a lasting prototype for its fascination with difference." Proceeding directly from this "conflation of biography, body and writing" in the construction and reception of Roy, Boehmer underlines a "critical inclination to regard as more culturally alive, interestingly authentic and intensively postcolonial than other kinds of international writing the extravagant realism and exuberant word-play associated with certain Indian writers, including Salman Rushdie and Arundhati Roy." Together with the focus on Roy's "taboo" subject matter, what it points to is a problematic replication of "inherited" perceptions of India as "multiple, extreme, scented, sensual, transgressive."

Characteristic of much of the scholarly focus on Roy's work to date, including that offered by Huggan and Boehmer, has been the issue of how the novel engages with a series of concerns that we might term postcolonial. Crucial to those works that explore the novel's engagement with the trajectories of India's colonial and postcolonial histories has been a focus on Roy's language. Where Michael Gorra suggests that, "the operatic intensity of the novel's emotions requires, if not Roy's linguistic excess, than at least her willingness to risk it" other critics, notably Aijaz Ahmad, Cynthia Van den Dreisen, Allesandro Monti, and Mary Condé locate Roy's linguistic strategies within the context of an attempt to rework the colonial roots of English in India. The purpose of this for Ahmad is the expression of "a provincial, vernacular culture without any effect of exoticism or estrangement, and without the book reading as translation." However, as I have also noted earlier, to use the term "provincial" to characterize what Roy is keen to illustrate as an historically hybridized culture that is and has been an active trader in a global system of cultural exchange, is something of a misnomer.

Dreisen, Monti, and Condé's essays on the subject of Roy's languages in the very uneven volume edited by R.K. Dhawan, *Arundhati Roy—The Novelist Extraordinary* (1999), read Roy's negotiation of an indigenous, Indian-English as an important subversion of the orders established by the colonial imposition of English such that the deployment of a reworked English offers both the novel's protagonists and Roy herself important oppositional modes for reinventing and reclaiming their own space and place in relation to Indian, British, and American cultures. Traversing similar territory but from a wider angle, and as part of a more general critique of the spectre of loss that haunts the novel, David Punter in his *Postcolonial Imaginings—Fictions of New World Order* (2000), elaborates on how the novel makes visible the languages displaced in the accession of English in the colonial and postcolonial era suggesting that "the language used to recount the story is haunted by the languages in which the protagonists might have told the tale—

had they had their own language, or indeed in this case *any* language, at their disposal." Continuing the focus on the politics of language in the novel, Nishi Chawla's "Beyond Arundhati Roy's 'Heart of Darkness': A Bakhtinian reading of *The God of Small Things*" in Dhawan's collection, argues that "for Roy as for Bakhtin, liberation is conceived in carnivalesque transgression as a flagrant defiance of bourgeois society; in high and low discourse and images of linguistic multiplicity and materiality" asserting that Roy's deployment of the language of the carnivalesque is part of the wider subversion of established values and authority in the novel. If the focus on Roy's languages can be located within the wider context of her postcolonial concerns, Victor Ramraj, in his essay; "Arundhati Roy's and Salman Rushdie's Postmodern India," also collected in Dhawan, is keen to switch the critical focus and to establish Roy's credentials as a chronicler of an India we might term postmodern *as well as* postcolonial. Indeed, Ramraj's reading persuasively argues that Roy, like Rushdie, is much more interested in excavating the value of the postmodern rather than the postcolonial as *the* lens through which contemporary India might be most productively understood and in this he offers, like Boehmer, Huggan, and Punter, further engaging lines of critical inquiry.

4

The Novel's Performance

Completed in May 1996 and launched in Delhi in April 1997, the success of *The God of Small Things* as a publishing phenomenon (with sales of over six million worldwide in forty different languages) has been the focus of almost as much, if not more, critical comment than the novel itself. Given the runaway success of *The God of Small Things* and the excess of comment that has focused on the narrative of Roy's discovery and rise to prominence, externally the role of international publishing, in creating, shaping, and maintaining a market for the Indo-Anglian novel cannot be underestimated. If the 1980s witnessed the second coming of the Indian novel (the first occurring in the 1930s) marked in no small part by the appearance of Salman Rushdie's Booker winning *Midnight's Children* (1981), then the crest of the new wave of interest in and criticism of the Indo-Anglian novel it initiated is nowhere more potently represented than in the publication, performance, and critical reception at a local and international level of Roy's novel.

Many critics including Aijaz Ahmad, Harish Trivedi, Fredric Jameson, and Graham Huggan have variously questioned the role of international publishing and the academic culture industry in creating a situation in which Indo-Anglian literature or Indian literature in English is, problematically, often read as a national literature (speaking to and for the multiplicity of communities and languages that come within the geopolitical boundaries of the nation) particularly in Western universities, despite the fact that for the most part, this literature is produced by an English-speaking minority from an affluent and cosmopolitan elite. For Harish Trivedi, writing in *Indian Literature* (September–October 1991), the dominant Indo-Anglian writers are guilty of a retreat into a metropolitan or cosmopolitan elitism that produces a literature "increasingly written by and for the English-knowing alone." What this conglomeration of forces produces, the above critics conclude, is a distorted and unrepresentative vision of both India and Indian history in the West—which once installed becomes the benchmark against which other Indo-Anglian writers are appraised and marketed. This is seen by several critics, like Graham Huggan and Jon Mee, as especially apparent in relation to the man widely accepted as kick starting the second wave of interest in the Indo-Anglian novel, and perhaps its most widely known and controversial spokesperson, Salman Rushdie, and in creating what has variously been termed "the Rushdie effect" or "Rushdieitis": that is the situation of Rushdie's work and *Midnight's Children* in particular as somehow representative and true of India's myriad histories and Indian literary history across thousands of years to the extent that, Michael Gorra claims, too much new Indian fiction has carried the birthmark of *Midnight's Children*. This is a claim reiterated in his assessment of Roy's novel for the *London Review of Books* (June 19, 1997). For the most part, Roy's novel has been set against the benchmark created by the critical reception and promotion of Rushdie. Indeed, such has been the novel's success that Roy's experience has been widely acknowledged as paving the way for the publication of a new generation of Indo-Anglian women first novelists in the late 1990s like Kiran Desai and Shauna Singh Baldwin. Like Rushdie, Roy too has been embroiled in controversy since the publication of *The God of Small Things*. This controversy has carried over and grown in her afterlife as political activist, all of which continue to have an impact on the sales of Roy's work. For example, her latest collection of critical essays, *Power Politics* (2001), has gone into several reprints after Roy's being held in contempt of court by the Indian Supreme Court in the latest saga of her battle against ongoing dam development in the Narmada valley.

After Rushdie's *Midnight's Children* and Vikram Seth's *A Suitable Boy*, the latter the focus of much critical comment because of the global advances it earned as for its epic proportions, the performance of Roy's novel according to Graham Huggan and following Padmia Mongia's deployment of the term must also be understood within the recent media-invented tradition of "Indo-chic." This is a label "global in its implications, coinciding with the recognition of India's emergence as a world economic power." "Indo-chic" as explained by Huggan, refers to the products of the globalization of Western-capitalist consumer culture, in which "India functions not just as a polyvalent cultural sign but as a highly mobile capital good." Saadia Toor's critical article, "Indo-Chic: The Cultural Politics of Consumption in Post-Liberalization India" argues that this rise in demand for Indian cultural artefacts is in no small part due to the demands of the Indian diaspora, particularly in the UK and North America. Toor compares the reception and promotion of films like Mira Nair's *Kamasutra* and Deepa Mehta's *Fire* with that of Roy's novel; all are for Toor gathered under the mantle of a neo-Orientalism that caters as much for emerging capitalist elites within India and a wider Indian diaspora as for other elements of Western audiences. It is true that *The God of Small Things* has in publishing terms performed particularly well in the West, especially in North

America and Britain. It has been high up in the American *Publishers Weekly* "Bestsellers of the Year" lists for three years between 1997 and 2000. It also performed well in India. The market for literature in English in India is small but expanding as Indo-Anglian fiction bankrolled by the lucrative global trade in "Indo-chic" generally from Bollywood to Bhangra finds itself in privileged competition with the literatures of India's sixteen official languages. Both Tarjun Tejpal at Roy's Indian publishers, IndiaInk, and P.N. Sukumar of Penguin India, have testified to the difficulty of selling literary fiction in a market as small as India's but in spite of this sales of Roy's novel have been buoyant, picking up particularly after it was awarded the Booker Prize and celebrity to boot. It has also performed well in translation. In France, for example, it has outperformed other often more established and garlanded Indo-Anglian novels like, for example, Rohinton Mistry's *A Fine Balance* (1996), which it outsold at about five to one. Mistry's novel had been equally well reviewed and was shortlisted for the Booker Prize in 1996. It had also won the IMPAC Dublin award and the Commonwealth Writers Prize for Best Book.

The outstanding performance of *The God of Small Things* against that achieved by Mistry is partly explainable by its general crossover appeal; it draws on several familiar strands from popular romance and melodrama, for example. But it must also be placed in the context of two events: the Golden Jubilee of India's Independence and the award of the Booker Prize, both of which were crucial to the increased visibility and recognition of Roy and *The God of Small Things* in 1997. The construction and repetition of the narrative of Roy's fairy-tale rise to prominence is essential to the star-making industry associated with the resurgence of interest in Indo-Anglian fiction in the 1990s. This star status was fed in Roy's case by the media celebration of the anniversary of India's fiftieth year of Independence from Britain in 1997. The Golden Jubilee provided the rationale for the launch of a number of critical surveys of India's contribution to literature in the period. In Britain and America, the established literary magazines, *Granta* and *The New Yorker* respectively offered their readers composite and often controversial pocketbook analyses of the state of India and Indo-Anglian writing generally, while Vintage Books, a subsidiary of Random House, rushed out *The Vintage Book of Indian Writing 1947–1997*, edited by Salman Rushdie and Elizabeth West, to capitalize on the renewed interest in India. The newly discovered and anthologized Roy featured in all three publications, shoulder to shoulder with Rushdie in *The New Yorker*, the combined effect being a further embedding of Roy within the media-constructed canon of Indo-Anglian fiction offered in each of these three features. Seen in this context, Roy's fairy-tale rise to public attention and acclaim is attributed by some commentators like Tarun J. Tejpal, writing in *The Guardian* (August 14, 1999), as the natural outcome of the "frenzy" of publishing interest in Indo-Anglian fiction after Anthony Cheetham's benchmark purchase of Vikram Seth's blockbuster, *A Suitable Boy*, in 1992. Representative of this embedding of Roy's discovery within the matrix of a "new gold-rush in the East" is Michael Gorra's opening gambit in the *London Review of Books*: "Here, with the cloud of a six-figure advance trailing behind her, comes Arundhati Roy." More tongue in cheek was *Private Eye* (October, 31 1997): "The God of Large Cheques by Arundhati Royalties."

The other major event to catapult Roy's novel even further up the bestseller list was its being awarded the Booker Prize in October 1997, the only first novel to do so since Keri Hulme's *The Bone People* won in 1985. The Booker Prize itself as Graham Huggan provocatively points out in *The Postcolonial Exotic — Marketing the Margins* (2000) has historically a rather dubious role in the mediation and canonization of ostensibly "third world literature" for a "first world market," adding further to the situation of Roy's text at the nexus of a complicated range of desires and anxieties which shape its appearance and journey in the world including its various audiences, publishers, judges, reviewers, and mediators inside and outside of the academy. In India, Roy's winning of the Booker was widely seen by the Indian media as injecting the book and the author with an unquestionable tincture of authority; adding further to sales of the novel and the narrative of celebrity. In Britain, response to the awarding of the Prize to Roy's novel in what was generally lamented as a rather unexciting year for the Booker, was more ambiguous, ranging from high praise to full scale demolition as represented by Carmen Callil's widely publicised verdict on the book and the decision as "execrable." Either way, the award has done much to increase both the visibility of the author and the performance of what was already a successful novel across the board and paved the way for phenomenal paperback sales in Britain and America in the following years.

5

Further Reading and Discussion Questions

This chapter complements the previous four by providing topics for discussion, suggestions for further reading and a series of questions that focus readers' thoughts on particular aspects of the novel. Some of these topics grow out of the issues discussed earlier, especially in Chapter 1 and 2.

DISCUSSION QUESTIONS

1. Roy has often suggested that she sees no distinction between her fiction writing and her journalism, specifically those essays on the critical issues facing India in the new millennium: the development of nuclear power, globalization, the ecological and environmental impact of India's continued commitment to big dam development, and more recently the rise of Islamic fundamentalism.

   Some of these essays are collected in *The Cost of Living* (1999), others have been published in *Power Politics* (2001) or in the Indian news magazines *Frontline* and *Outlook*, while two articles on the September 11th crisis have been published in *The Guardian* (UK) and can be read at *www. theguardianonline.co.uk*.

What do you think are the connections between Roy's fiction and her criticism? In what ways might the critical work further the series of anxieties, concerns, or themes delineated in *The God of Small Things*?

2. Critics have often stressed the importance of Roy's debt to Salman Rushdie, notably the epic *Midnight's Children*. The critic, Michael Gorra, for example, sees Roy's style as overly influenced by Rushdie's. What features of Rushdie's fictions recur in Roy's novel? What elements of Rushdie's critical reflections, some of which are collected in his *Imaginary Homelands: Essays and Criticism 1981–1991* (1991) illuminate, if at all, our reading of Roy's texts (novel and critical essays)?

   Victor Ramraj has suggested that Roy like Rushdie is interested in examining India through the lens of the postmodern? In what ways might their visions of India be termed postmodern? How and in what ways might Roy's fiction be termed postmodern?

   Starting points for readers interested in thinking about Roy's text in terms of postmodernism and postmodernity could include Tim Woods' *Beginning Postmodernism* (1999). More advanced investigators might find useful, the guides to postmodernist fiction and theory offered by Linda Hutcheon in *A Poetics of Postmodernism* (1988) and *The Politics of Postmodernism* (1989) and Brian McHale in *Postmodernist Fiction* (1987).

3. Roy's novel can be termed postcolonial in that it actively returns to and interrogates the legacy of India's colonial and postcolonial histories. How does it do so? How might one compare it

with other novels that deal with the vexed question of India's postcolonial identity?

Examples for comparison could include Salman Rushdie's *The Moor's Last Sigh* (1995), Nayantara Sahgal's *Rich Like Us* (1983), Anita Desai's *Clear Light of Day* (1980), and Vikram Chandra's *Red Earth and Pouring Rain* (1995).

Useful starting points for readers interested in thinking about postcolonialism generally and India specifically include Bill Ashcroft et al. *The Empire Writes Back: Theory and Practice in Post-Colonial Literatures* (1989), John McLeod's *Beginning Postcolonialism* (2000), Elleke Boehmer's *Colonial and Postcolonial Literature — Migrant Metaphors* (1995), Dennis Walder's *Post-colonial Literatures in English* (1998).

4. The theme of caste, its unities, divisions, collusions, and complicities are uppermost in *The God of Small Things*?

How and in what ways does caste impact upon the lives of Roy's protagonists?

How are questions of caste further complicated by their intersection with issues of class and gender in the novel?

How might Roy's reading of caste in *The God of Small Things* be compared with that offered in her two critical articles about Phoolan Devi and the representation of Devi's story in Shekar Kapur's film, *Bandit Queen* (1994)?

5. In what ways does Roy's novel explore the issue of belonging, particularly the question of belonging to more than one culture or more than one nation?

How might it compare, for example, with other writings that explore the dynamics of belonging in the post-colonial era?

Some comparative examples could include Sunetra Gupta's *Memories of Rain* (1992), Bharati Mukherjee's *The Middleman and Other Stories* (1988), Zadie Smith's *White Teeth* (2000),

Bernardine Evaristo's *Lara* (1997), Hanif Kureishi's *The Buddha of Suburbia* (1991) and *The Black Album* (1995), or Jumpha Lahiri's *Interpreter of Maladies* (1999).

6. Consider Roy's representation of Pappachi as colonial servant. Once an active participant in the administration of British India, he must renegotiate his understanding of his space and place in the world in the aftermath of Independence and Partition. How successful is he in doing so?

How might one compare Roy's representation of Pappachi with other novels in which the ambivalent figure of the colonial servant features prominently like Upamanyu Chatterjee's *English, August: An Indian Story* (1988) or Nayantara Sahgal's *Rich Like Us* (1983)?

7. Many Indo-Anglian writers, including Roy, explore the ongoing role of myth in the shaping of modern India, particularly those stories related in the great epics, the *Mahabaratha* and the *Ramayana*, the storehouses of Indian tradition. Where and how does Roy's text draw on Indian myth? What are the significance of the myths Roy draws upon in her narrative of love, betrayal, and entrapment in *The God of Small Things*?

How might Roy's use of myth compare with other powerful reinventions and dissections of the role of myth in the formation and maintenance of structures of power in Indian society, like that offered in Githa Hariharan's *The Thousand Faces of Night* (1992) or Vikram Chandra's *Red Earth and Pouring Rain* (1995)?

Useful starting points for thinking about the role of myth in Indian culture include Sara S. Mitter's *Dharma's Daughters: Contemporary Indian Women and Hindu Culture* (1991), Shashi Deshpande's "The Indian Woman — Stereotypes, Images and Realities" at *http://ch.8m.com/shashi.htm* and Anita

Desai's "A Secret Connivance" in the *Times Literary Supplement* (September, 14 1990).

How might Roy's reworking of the power of myth compare with that offered by non Indo-Anglian writers like Angela Carter in *The Passion of New Eve* or Margaret Atwood in *The Robber Bride* (1994) or Dorothy Porter in *Crete* (1996)?

8. What is the significance of Roy's title? Who or what is the God of Small Things? What role do the small things have in the larger story the novel has to tell?

9. Why do you think Roy uses the child's eye point of view for substantial sections of the novel? What kind of vision of childhood does Roy offer in the novel?

   You might find it useful to compare Roy's novel with others in which the child's eye point of view or the inner life of the child features prominently like Anita Desai's *Fire on the Mountain* (1977), Githa Hariharan *The Thousand Faces of Night* (1992), Meera Syal's *Anita and Me* (1997), or Seamus Deane's *Reading in the Dark* (1996).

10. Roy's refashioning of English has been the subject of much critical comment. How and in what ways does Roy depart from standard English? Why? What is the overall effect of Roy's reworking of English in *The God of Small Things*?

    In what ways might the question of language be a concern she shares with a number of other postcolonial writers? Can you think of other writers who are consciously refashioning English in order to make it fit the specificities of their own history, culture and experience? Do they employ similar or different techniques for reinventing English?

11. What does Roy's novel have to tell us about the impact of globalization on India? What are the advantages and disadvantages brought about by this experience?

To what extent is Roy's exploration of India's space and place in a global world complicated and/or promulgated by the already hybridized nature of Indian culture and/or India's long history of colonization?

12. What is significant about Chacko's experience of Oxford? What vision of the migrant do we get in the representation of Chacko's and Rahel's experiences abroad? How do Chacko and Rahel's experience of migrancy compare?

What are the attractions and tensions of an Oxford education for the Indian student as elucidated in novels like Roy's, Amit Chaudhuri's *Afternoon Raag* (1993) and/or Nayantara Sahgal's *Rich Like Us* (1983)?

What might these representations reveal to us about what characterizes the experience of a migrant?

In what ways does the condition of migrancy exposed in these texts construct modes of existence and ways of seeing that last beyond the actual journey between countries?

Useful starting points for thinking about the issue of migrant and diasporic identities generally are Robin Cohen's *Global Diasporas: An Introduction* (1997) and Avtar Brah's *Cartographies of Diaspora: Contesting Identities* (1997).

13. Roy's novel focuses on the issue of love across the divides of race, caste, and nationality What vision of these relationships are we offered?

How might they compare with similar explorations in Zadie Smith's *White Teeth*, Bernardine Evaristo's *Lara* or Brian Friel's *Translations* (1981)?

FURTHER READING

If you liked *The God of Small Things* you might also enjoy the
following:

Anita Desai's *Fire on the Mountain, Clear Light of Day*, and
Fasting, Feasting;

Nayantara Sahgal's *Rich Like Us;*

Michael Ondaatje's *Running in the Family, In the Skin of a
Lion*, and *Anil's Ghost*

Vikram Chandra's *Red Earth and Pouring Rain*

Jhumpa Lahiri's *Interpreter of Maladies*

Amit Chaudhuri's *Afternoon Raag*

I. Allan Sealy's *The Everest Hotel*

Romesh Guneskera's *Reef*

Shyam Selvadurai's *Funny Boy* and *The Cinnamon Gardens*

Amitav Ghosh's *The Shadow Lines* and *The Glass Palace*

Bapsi Sidhwa's *Ice-Candy-Man/Cracking India*

Interviews and Websites

Roy is the subject of several published interviews, some of which are cited
in earlier chapters of this book.

Alok Roi in *The Sunday Review* of *The Times of India* (April 1997)

Taisa Abraham in *Ariel: A Review of International English Literature* 29:1
(January 1998)

The following feature articles have also been consulted:

Maya Jaggi, "An Unsuitable Girl". *The Guardian Weekend* (May 24th,
1997), "Hype, Hype Hooray." *The Irish Times* (October 18th, 1997)

Madeleine Bunting, "Dambuster," *The Guardian Weekend* (July 28th, 2001)

Bill Buford, "Declarations of Independence: Why Are There Suddenly So Many Indian Novelists?" *The New Yorker* (June 23–30th, 1997)
Additional useful interviews relating to the novel and Roy's more recent political engagements may be located on the worldwide web. See, for example:

Roy's *Salon* interview with Reena Jana (Sept 1997) at *http: www.salonmagazine.com/sept97//00roy.html*

N. Ram's "Scimitars in The Sun" at the Indian news magazine, *Frontline* 18:1 (Jan 6–19 2001) at *www.frontlineonline.com*

David Barsamian in the April 2001 issue of *The Progressive* at *http://www.progressive.org/intv0401.html* and interview at *www. WordsWorth.com* (June 1997)

The most organized and useful of the websites devoted to Arundhati Roy is Jon Simmons' at *http://website.lineone.net/~jon.simmons/roy.* This is regularly updated and contains useful links to many resources.

Bibliography

Works by Arundhati Roy

The God of Small Things. London: Flamingo, 1997.
The Cost of Living. London: Flamingo, 1999.
Power Politics. Cambridge, Mass: South End Press, 2001.

Select Criticism

Ashcroft, Bill. et al. *The Empire Writes Back: Theory and Practice in Post-Colonial Literatures*. London and New York: Routledge, 1989.

Bhabha, Homi. *The Location of Culture*. London and New York: Routledge, 1994.

Boehmer, Elleke. "East Is East and South Is South: The Cases of Sarojini Naidu and Arundhati Roy." *Women: A cultural review*. 11:1/2, 2000: 61–70.

Bunting, Madeleine. "Dambuster." *The Guardian Weekend*. July, 28 2001: 20–26.

Chandra, Vikram. "The Cult of Authenticity." *The Boston Review*. February–March 2000, *http://bostonreview.mit.edu/BR25.1/chandra.html*.

Chauduri, Amit. "The Construction of the Indian Novel in English." *The*

Picador Book of Modern Indian Literature. London: Macmillan, 2001. xxiii–xxxi.

Chew, Shirley. Review of *The God of Small Things. Times Literary Supplement.* (May 30, 1997).

Condé, Mary. "Finding a New Independence: Indian Women Writing in English." In Kathleen Firth and Felicity Hand, eds. *India: Fifty Years After Independence.* Leeds: Peepal Tree, 2001: 24–35.

Davey, Frank and Nichol, bp. *Robert Kroetsch: Essays.* Toronto: Open Letter, 1983.

Desai, Anita. "A Secret Connivance." In *Times Literary Supplement.* September, 14 1990.

Deshpande, Shashi. "Them and Us." Shirley Chew and Anna Rutherford, eds, *Unbecoming Daughters of the Empire.* Hebden Bridge: Dangaroo Press, 1993: 101–107.

Dinnage, Rosemary. "Out of the Ruins." *The New York Review.* (August 14, 1997): 16–17.

Dreisen, Cynthia Vanden. "When Language Dances: The Subversive Power of Roy's Text in *The God of Small Things.*" In R.K. Dhawan, ed. *Arundhati Roy: The Novelist Extraordinary.* London: Sangam Books, 1999: 365–377.

Fernandes, Leela. "Reading India's 'Bandit Queen': A Trans/national Feminist Perspective on the Discrepancies of Representation." *Signs: Journal of Women in Culture and Society.* 25:1, 1999:123–152.

Gandhi, Leela. "Indo-Anglian Fiction: Writing India, Elite Aesthetics, and the Rise of the 'Stephanian' Novel." *Australian Humanities Review.* November, 8 1997–January 1998) *http://lib.latrobe.edu.au/AHR/archive* Issue-November-1997/gandhi.html.

Gorra, Michael. "Living in the Aftermath." *London Review of Books.* (June 19, 1997): 22-23.

Huggan, Graham. *The Postcolonial Exotic: Marketing the Margins.* London and New York: Routledge, 2001: 58–83.

Jaggi, Maya. "An Unsuitable Girl." *The Guardian Weekend.* (May 24, 1997): 12–18.

Kakutani, Michiko. *New York Times.* (June 3, 1997): 20.

Mee, Jon. "After midnight: the Indian novel in English of the 80s and 90s." *Postcolonial Studies*. 1:1 (1998): 127–141.

Prasad, G.J.V. "Writing Translation—The Strange Case of the Indian English novel." Susan Bassenet and Harish Trivedi, eds. *Post-Colonial Translation: Theory and Practice*. London and New York: Routledge, 1999. 41–58.

Punter, David. *Postcolonial Imaginings, Fictions of a New World Order*. Edinburgh: Edinburgh University Press, 2000.

Rajan, Rajeswari Sunder. *Real and Imagined Women—Gender, Culture and Postcolonialism*. London and New York: Routledge, 1993.

Rushdie, Salman and West, Elizabeth. Eds. *The Vintage Book of Indian Writing 1947–1997*. London:Vintage, 1997.

Sahgal, Nayantara. "Some Thoughts on the Puzzle of Identity." *Journal of Commonwealth Literature*. 28/1, 1993: 3–15.

Spivak, Gayatri. "Can the Subaltern Speak?" In *Marxism and the Interpretation of Culture*. Cary Nelson and Lawrence Grossberg, eds. Urbana: University of Illinois Press, 1988: 271–313.

Trivedi, Harish. "The St. Stephen's Factor." *Indian Literature*. 145, 1991: 183–187.

Walder, Dennis. *Post-colonial Literatures in English: History, Language, Theory*. Oxford: Blackwell, 1998.

Zarilli, Phillip B. *Kathakali dance-drama*. London and New York: Routledge, 2000.